CONTENTS

INTRODUCTION

Welcome to a journey through some of the overlooked and unreported ghost stories from Edinburgh and across Scotland.

In this book, we will explore some of my favourite overlooked tales of the paranormal that continue to haunt the streets and landscapes of these historic locations. I will also share some stories that have never been published before, documenting these accounts for the first time and shedding light on intriguing and lesser-known aspects of their history.

Scotland's untamed, evocative landscapes and rich history are a blend of mystery and folklore. From ancient castles perched on mist-covered hills overlooking atmospheric glens to remote, windswept moors steeped in legend, every corner of this enchanting country holds supernatural secrets waiting to be discovered.

Here, tales of ghosts, spirits, and otherworldly beings have been passed down through generations, woven into the fabric of its culture and the composition of its people. As we explore the overlooked and unreported ghost stories of Edinburgh and Scotland, we are drawn deeper into the mystique of this intriguing land, where myth and reality often intertwine, and the past whispers its secrets to those who listen closely.

In recent years, Scotland has become a hotspot for both conventional and paranormal tourism, with Edinburgh being the focal point of this influx. Legendary locations like Greyfriars Kirkyard, Glamis Castle, and the Edinburgh Vaults have brought a renewed interest in Scotland's haunted history, stealing the limelight from other, arguably more interesting and terrifying hauntings, such as those at Buckingham Terrace and the Seton Haunting in the New Town of Edinburgh.

Groundbreaking television programmes such as *Most Haunted* and *Ghost Adventures* have frequently visited Scotland, further fuelling fascination with its supernatural stories. These programmes have inspired amateur ghost-hunting groups to spring up, eager to explore the dark, eerie corners of Scotland and uncover its spectral secrets. Moreover, interest in these stories remains high, as evidenced by the success of my YouTube channel, Eerie Edinburgh, which features many of these haunting tales and has garnered a dedicated following. With each upload, viewers from around the world are drawn to hear a captivating blend of Scotland's colourful history and countless ghostly mysteries, many of which are direct experiences shared with me by eager viewers of the channel.

With the growth of ghost hunting and the boom in self-made ghost-hunting programme availability, more and more people feel comfortable enough to come forward with their own encounters. In fact, this book contains some stories that have been recounted directly to me from people who felt they had to get their stories out. They are not the only people to experience the paranormal. I too have had my own unusual events happen to me, most notably in August 2006 when I visited the small Isle of Gigha, a short ferry ride from the Mull of Kintyre on the west coast of mainland Scotland.

At that time, I was in my mid-thirties and a proud, first-time father to my nine-month-old son, Gabriel, and happily engaged to my future ex-wife, Helena, who, among many other things, was a talented professional photographer. She had been commissioned by the people of Gigha to visit the island and take pictures for their new website. This website would help promote the island after the community bought it from the previous owner, Derek Holt.

As part of the arrangement, our accommodation was provided for free. We would be staying the weekend at a place near the beach called the Ferryman's Cottage.

The cottage is charming but unremarkable, set in a fantastic location literally a two-minute walk from the beach. When we parked in the drive at the front of the cottage, we stopped to admire this little building that would be home for the next couple of nights. It's a good size, with two upstairs bedrooms, an upstairs toilet, and the kitchen and living room on the ground floor. The staircase is in the centre of the house as you walk in. The cottage has self-contained gardens, so we let Gabriel out for a quick crawl on the grass while we stretched our legs and had a quick look around outside.

After unpacking the car and getting Gabriel to sleep, I made some lunch. The kitchen, relatively small and narrow, had the sink on the right as you walked in, and the microwave towards the end, with storage cupboards on the wall towards the back of the room.

The kitchen had pretty basic amenities, but everything you'd need for a weekend away. I was washing up some pots in the sink, and to make space, I moved the toaster, which was to my left, further down the counter. After a minute or so of washing, I noticed out of the corner of my eye that the toaster moved. Not a big, sudden, loud movement, but a slow slide across the counter, I'd guess two inches or so. Enough for me to see it and to hear it.

I stopped what I was doing and moved for a closer look, thinking when I'd moved it, I'd somehow coiled the wires up, and it was their releasing the tension that had caused the toaster to move. There was no water underneath the toaster, so it couldn't have been sliding, and the wire looked fine, so I was left a little confused but still sure it had to be down to tension in the wire. Given I'd 'found' the reason for the toaster moving, I decided it wasn't worth mentioning to Helena, as I didn't want to upset her, but I sensed an uneasy atmosphere in the cottage, not necessarily sinister, but definitely uncomfortable.

We had been awake since about 5.00am due to the long drive, and feeling weary, I headed to the main bedroom upstairs, situated on the left side at the top of the stairs.

The bathroom was straight ahead, with a typical period design featuring a half-wood and half-frosted-glass door. To the right of the bathroom was the second bedroom, where we found an old wooden cot that seemed perfect for Gabriel. The overall decor of the house, while pleasant, emitted a vibe of a bygone era.

Although the bedroom felt comfortable, I found it difficult to settle and sleep. Eventually, I decided to get up and return downstairs. I half-expected to find a nervous Helena waiting by the car, ready to leave, as she had grown uneasy with the place. However, everything seemed normal. Helena did enquire about what I was searching for when she returned from the bathroom. She mentioned seeing me walk past the bathroom door from the main bedroom into the spare room where the cot was, but I hadn't done so. Not wanting to alarm her, especially since we had nowhere else to go on the island, I simply brushed it off, attributing it to restlessness.

As bedtime approached, we found ourselves discussing where to sleep, subtly avoiding the topic of going upstairs, which we both clearly did not want to do. Eventually, we agreed to sleep in the living room, where the rather dated TV was located, neither of us wanting to venture upstairs. We prepared makeshift beds on the floor, with Gabriel sleeping in the middle. Concerned about his safety – given he was a curious child who crawled everywhere – we barricaded the foot of the stairs using the coffee table, the car parcel shelf, and numerous spare pillows. Despite our unease, the cottage had a definite atmosphere that pervaded the air, we stayed together in the living room to avoid alarming each other.

We managed to get some sleep, or at least as much as Gabriel's crawling, kicking and crying would allow. The next day, despite the dismal weather, we set out to take as many pictures of the island for the website as we could. Although the conditions were challenging, Helena persevered and did her best. Anticipating better weather the following day, we postponed photographing the cottage and waited for better light. Sunday arrived, and it was time to load up the car and head home. My task was tidying up the cottage so Helena could take pictures – but we decided it was best if we left the barricade in place for now as, even though it was daylight, we still felt uncomfortable with the upstairs. During packing, panic struck when we realised we couldn't hear Gabriel. We searched everywhere, the car, behind the couch and the fenced-in garden, but he wasn't in sight. The realisation hit us that he must be upstairs, yet the barricade we set up remained undisturbed, leaving us puzzled about how he could have got up there unnoticed.

I quickly moved the coffee table and hurried upstairs to find Gabriel safe and oblivious to our distress. Despite my fear of the upstairs area, there he was, crawling around without a care in the world.

This, for us, was the final straw, so we quickly packed up and left the cottage, catching an earlier ferry than originally planned. Later, as we sat in the car, we shared our discomfort about the cottage. Both Helena and I recounted our strange experiences – me with the moving toaster and her with a passing shadow in the bathroom. Although separate incidents, we both felt something was off.

After Helena uploaded her photos, disappointment clouded her mood due to the weather's impact on the shots. Yet the pictures of the Ferryman's Cottage revealed something eerie – a light in the unlit toilet. It wasn't a reflection on the glass nor the bathroom light. However, the most chilling picture was the last one we opened: an image showing the ghostly outline of a boy in the porch window, surrounded by an iridescent aura.

Unfortunately, we lost these images when my old PC crashed, leaving us, as is usually the case with accounts like this, unable to prove our experiences.

To this day, we remain puzzled about how Gabriel bypassed the barricade unnoticed.

These inexplicable occurrences are not unique to isolated incidents like Gabriel's. From the ancient cobbled streets of the country's capital, Edinburgh, to the rugged landscapes of the

Highlands and islands, Scotland harbours a mosaic of phantom inhabitants, each waiting to be uncovered by those curious enough to seek them out.

I'm convinced that thousands more stories like mine go unreported, overshadowed by the attention given to Greyfriars and the Edinburgh Vaults. Over the years, I've talked to hundreds of people about ghosts and mysterious occurrences, and most greet me with a puzzled, disbelieving look, and the rest look at me like I'm crazy. However, disbelief often turns to belief after personal encounters. For instance, a colleague of mine, initially sceptical, explained that he didn't believe in ghosts, but he was perplexed by the recurring sight of an 'old man' in his bedroom mirror.

This book will present six stories in each section, spanning from Edinburgh's Old Town to the wider Edinburgh region, and then on to various locations across the length and breadth of Scotland. Our journey begins in Edinburgh, a city steeped in millennia of history, where we'll explore the supernatural encounters along the Royal Mile, known as Edinburgh's "Old Town". Here, we'll delve into intriguing locations like Chessels Court, Queensberry House, and the Museum of Edinburgh.

What makes these stories compelling is not just the ghostly phenomena but the rich history of the land, the people, the families, and the buildings involved. Understanding this history adds depth to the tales, sometimes revealing the context behind the hauntings. Along with the ghost stories, we'll explore the historical narratives that intertwine with these supernatural events, providing a fuller picture of why these places might be haunted. I firmly believe that if you want to understand a haunting, you have to understand the history.

With this approach in mind, we'll continue our exploration by venturing into the wider Edinburgh area to revisit some of the most remarkable forgotten hauntings, such as those of Blacket Place and the ancient mysteries of Craigmillar Castle.

Expanding our haunted horizons, we'll journey into the mystical, ancient landscapes surrounding Liarn Farm on the shores of Loch Rannoch and the foreboding depths of Ballechin House in Perth, once acclaimed as the "most haunted house in Scotland". In Bearsden, Glasgow, we feature a truly chilling tale of an encounter with restless spirits in an old Georgian townhouse. Meanwhile, the rugged, remote terrain of Sligachan on the Isle of Skye is filled with stories of long-forgotten clan warfare and a phantom car that haunts the island's roads.

Join us as we uncover the hidden secrets scattered across Scotland's haunted landscapes. Prepare to be captivated by spectral sightings, enigmatic apparitions, and inexplicable events, as we shed light on the unreported and overlooked ghostly narratives that lie just beyond the ordinary.

PART ONE
EERIE EDINBURGH
THE OLD TOWN

Welcome to part one of our exploration into the haunting depths of Edinburgh's Old Town.

Where else could we start but the Royal Mile? Often referred to as the Old Town, this timeless thoroughfare stands as a living testament to Edinburgh's rich and intriguing, often dark and macabre history. The Royal Mile stretches from the iconic and ancient fortress of Edinburgh Castle, perched atop its volcanic crag, down to the majestic Holyrood Palace at the foot of Arthur's Seat. This historic mile-long stretch encapsulates centuries of stories, from the grandeur of royal processions to the turbulent events of the Scottish Reformation.

The Reformation transformed the Royal Mile by shifting the focus from Catholicism to Protestantism, leading to significant changes in religious practices and institutions. Churches were restructured to align with Protestant beliefs, and many religious buildings were repurposed. This shift influenced the social and political dynamics of the area, promoting education and literacy and contributing to a more informed and engaged populace. The physical landscape of the Royal Mile was altered as religious iconography and practices were replaced with those that aligned with Protestant values, leaving a lasting impact on the cultural and historical fabric of the area.

But beneath the Royal Mile's picturesque facade lies a darker past. In centuries gone by, the Royal Mile was not the bustling tourist destination it is today, filled with cafes and shops selling Harry Potter memorabilia, but rather a teeming, crowded thoroughfare where most of the city's sixty thousand residents once lived in abject squalor and filth. With space at a premium and sanitation virtually non-existent unless you could afford it, the then city planners were forced to build upwards, creating the towering tenements and narrow closes that still define the area's world-famous skyline. Some of these tenements reached up to fourteen stories high, with the top floors made of wood since the technology to build stone structures that tall wasn't available at the time. This meant the wealthier occupants lived on the lower floors, where fireplaces could be constructed, while those less fortunate were crammed into the wooden upper floors, unable to heat their living spaces during the cold winter months.

The dense urban layout was necessary due to the surrounding marshlands, lochs, rivers, and the constant fear of invasion. The Flodden Wall, built in the sixteenth century after the Scottish Army's defeat by the English in the disastrous Battle of Flodden in 1513, served as a crucial defensive measure. Constructed to safeguard the city and its inhabitants against potential English invasions, this formidable fortification encircled Edinburgh, shaping its architectural landscape and urban development for centuries to come. For the keen-eyed explorers out there, you can still find remnants of the wall in some of the older areas of the city. As someone who enjoys taking self-guided tours of the haunted hotspots along the Royal Mile, visiting places like the Canongate, retracing the steps of the famous ghostly piper of Edinburgh Castle, and my taking in the impressive aura of my favourite haunted house, Queensberry House, I find the history and stories of these places fascinating.

Unfortunately, violence was an everyday occurrence along the Mile's narrow, winding closes and in its straw-covered drinking dens. Infamous characters such as the body snatchers Burke and Hare, who murdered people to sell their bodies to medical schools, the thief and respected cabinetmaker Deacon Brodie, who led a double life of crime, and Major Thomas Weir, now dubbed the 'Wizard of the West Bow' for his reputed practice of dark arts, all once called this historic street home.

Despite its humble beginnings, the Royal Mile has evolved into a vibrant hub of culture and history, with its centuries-old buildings now housing museums, shops, and eateries. Yet beneath the surface, the echoes of its darker past still resonate, adding depth and character to this iconic Edinburgh landmark.

Here, amidst the cobbled streets and historic buildings, lie countless tales of ghosts and hauntings – some known, some less well-known, and some forgotten. These hauntings extend below the streets to world-famous places like Mary King's Close and the Blair and Niddry Street Vaults, where the supernatural lingers in the dark.

Join us as we wander through shadowy alleyways and hidden closes, meeting otherworldly inhabitants from days gone by and hearing whispers of haunting encounters and chilling apparitions that linger in the air. From the depths of the Royal Mile to the secluded corners of the Grassmarket, prepare to delve into the haunted history of Edinburgh's oldest and most mysterious district.

CHAPTER 1
EDINBURGH CASTLE
THE GOVERNOR'S HOUSE

AMID EDINBURGH'S ICONIC SKYLINE, one structure commands attention above all: Edinburgh Castle. The Old Town skyline, with its mediaeval layout and historic buildings, is protected as part of the UNESCO World Heritage Site designation. This status ensures that the architectural and historical significance of the area is preserved, with strict regulations on new developments and alterations to existing structures. Edinburgh takes its skyline so seriously that it is safeguarded to maintain its unique charm and historical integrity.

Sitting atop Castle Rock, this historic site exudes a tangible connection to the past, having watched over the city for countless generations. Castle Rock is among three dormant volcanoes in Edinburgh, including Arthur's Seat and Calton Hill. It took shape approximately 350 million years ago during the Carboniferous period, a relic of Edinburgh's geological history. The rock itself formed from cooled volcanic magma, creating dolerite over millennia.

The story of Edinburgh Castle begins around 600 CE, when the Celts, notably the Votadini tribe, inhabited the rocky outcrop, establishing Eeden's Hill Fort on Castle Rock. The Votadini's domain stretched from the Firth of Forth to the northeast reaches of modern England, with their stronghold believed to have been at Traprain Law, a mere twenty-three miles from Edinburgh.

Construction of Edinburgh Castle, as it stands today, began in the eleventh century with the building of St Margaret's Chapel, a masterpiece of mediaeval craftsmanship. Over the centuries, the castle underwent numerous expansions, from the construction of St David's Tower to the formidable Half Moon Battery, each adding to its rich historical fabric.

As Britain's most besieged stronghold, Edinburgh Castle endured twenty-three assaults throughout its tumultuous past, leaving an indelible mark on its surroundings. The echoes of conflict and strife infuse the castle and its environs with an undeniable aura of the supernatural.

Edinburgh's architectural landscape reflects its substantial history, with thirteen castles found within the city limits bearing witness to centuries of triumphs and tragedies. From the ancient ruins of Barnbougle to the regal splendour of Bavelaw Castle, each structure tells a tale of Scotland's past and the people who lived there.

Craigmillar Castle, once the refuge of Mary Queen of Scots, may hold secret hidden passageways linking it to Holyrood Palace, while the imposing Cramond Tower stands watch over the waters of the Firth of Forth.

It's fascinating to note that the history of these ancient seats of power isn't confined to books alone. Some witness their most dreadful and ruinous events replayed even into modern times, with ghostly figures and uncanny events occurring regularly.

Many historical events have taken place behind its thick stone walls. *Game of Thrones* fans may be surprised to learn that "the Red Wedding" is, in part, based on an event that took place in 1440 that became known as "the black dinner".

On 24 November 1440, the fifteen-year-old Earl of Douglas and his brother, David, were invited to have dinner at Edinburgh Castle by William Crichton.

After the feast began, it's said a bull's head was placed in the centre of the table, the young brothers were set upon and then seized by Crichton's men, unjustly accused of treason and later executed, their heads later displayed on Castle Hill.

In addition to its historical tales, the castle boasts a collection of stories that veer into the realm of the macabre and the supernatural. Among these, one particular encounter centres around the Governor's House.

This overlooked story leads us into the depths of the castle, where tales of ghostly encounters and unexplainable events persist. Today, our focus is on the Governor's House, inviting us to delve into its dim passageways and reveal the mysteries hidden within.

The current Governor's House was built around 1740, but a more ancient building is said to have stood on the site long before the new house was built.

Our story starts around 130 years ago when a soldier named Robert Eliot Westwood was stationed in the castle, staying in the Governor's House. Robert, an instructor in the Royal Engineers, shared the lodging with his friend named Tom. Both men had known each other for a while, and neither were prone to believe some of their fellow soldiers' tales of supernatural events in their ancient surroundings that happened within the castle walls. He put any such down to campfire stories and too much whiskey. Before joining the army, Tom had lived a previous life as a schoolmaster in England, where he had developed a strong and unwavering belief system.

After sharing the usual stories with their comrades and hearing well-crafted tales of ghosts and things that go bump in the night, Tom and Robert headed to their second-floor lodgings for the night. Robert, intrigued by some of the stories, recounted several to the sceptical Tom, who, having no personal experiences with such phenomena, promptly brushed them aside. Nonetheless, despite Tom's scepticism, he ensured that all the doors to their lodgings were securely locked.

Once satisfied the room was secure, Tom had climbed into his bunk, and then both men noticed Tom had forgotten to blow out the candle. Robert warned him, "One day you'll be burned in your bed. Be sure to put that candle out so that a tragedy like that does not happen to us," at which Robert blew out the candle, and they both settled down to sleep.

After a while, a terrific noise shocked them awake. The noise was unmistakable; it was the securely locked and bolted front door into the Governor's House hitting against the wall as if flung open by some massive force.

A few seconds of silence followed before footsteps were heard, bounding footsteps running up the stairs, towards their lodgings. Tom gasped in fright, unable to rationalise what was happening and the speed at which events unfolded. He turned to look at Robert, grabbing his hand in fear just as the door to their lodgings was thrown open and a gust of wind swept through the room as the footsteps came straight for the terrified soldiers, and then as suddenly as it all started, the commotion stopped.

As the events unfolded, both men felt a palpable sense of malevolence descend upon the room, creating a sinister atmosphere. However, as swiftly as it had appeared, this ominous presence began to dissipate, gradually fading away until silence enveloped the space once more, leaving an unsettling calm in its wake.

Aware that their room door was open, Tom and Robert realised that the main door to the house also had to be open, so they made their way downstairs to secure it.

Upon reaching the heavy main door, they were shocked and confused to see it wide open, but its bolts were still shot with no damage to the fittings.

Fearful of what force could have done this and for their sanity, they quickly secured the door, made sure the bolts were in place and went back to try to get some sleep.

A few hours passed, and again they were awoken with a start by the sounds of the front door crashing against the wall, the heavy footsteps on the stairs, the bedroom door being flung open, followed by gusts of wind and the feeling of evil, then the footsteps rushing over toward them, then the silence.

As before, they nervously made their way down the stairs to find the main door open and the bolts still in place.

Again, they closed the door securely and made their way back to their lodgings, this time deciding it might be best to stay awake rather than try to get some sleep, and this they did.

As dawn broke, the men recounted their unbelievable tale to their fellow soldiers, expecting to be laughed out of the castle, but instead they were told about something that might have explained their supernatural experience.

The evening of the events was the two-hundred-year anniversary of a tragic incident.

During the Jacobite rising of 1689, the Duke of Gordon, the then governor of Edinburgh, fearing the castle would come again under siege, had made arrangements for his family to travel across the Firth of Forth, to Fife.

His steward was charged with his family's protection and had sworn to do so; he could not protect them from the forces of nature, however.

During the short voyage, all aboard the ship except the steward were lost when a tempest arose and overwhelmed the vessel.

After reaching the safety of the Edinburgh shore, the steward made his way back to the castle as fast as his horse could carry him. On reaching the governor's house, he threw open the heavy front door, ran up the stairs to the second-floor room and approached the governor's room, throwing open the door and then relaying the events that had happened to the governor's family.

On hearing this news, the governor, in a fit of rage and heartbreak, is said to have killed the steward on the very spot where the footsteps stopped, right next to where the two soldiers slept.

Although Edinburgh Castle is famously haunted by numerous ghosts and spirits, such as the apparition of Major John "Bonnie Dundee" Claverhouse and the headless drummer whose staccato beats echo from the castle courtyard, the story of the spectral steward is one that has almost completely faded from memory.

Perhaps this is because it has only been officially reported on one occasion, as far as I have been able to find. Or perhaps it lacks the evocative allure of other well-known hauntings – there's no classic apparition of a jilted "Lady in Black" lover or a malevolent presence like Mr Boots, who is said to now haunt many of the underground vaults. Nevertheless, its rarity and mystery add an intriguing layer to the castle's ghostly lore.

To me, this is an encounter that has many of the classic traits of a good ghost story. It's set amidst a historical location, with phantom footsteps and other unexplained phenomena adding to its chilling atmosphere. Its catalyst was an historical tragedy that echoes through the centuries, leaving behind a lingering sense of sorrow and unrest. While it may not boast the sensationalism of other well-known hauntings, its rarity and mystery make it worthy of inclusion and only serve to deepen the intrigue surrounding Edinburgh Castle's ghostly lore.

CHAPTER 2
CHESSEL'S COURT

Old Edinburgh is often described as looking like fishbones from above: the Royal Mile forms the spine, with numerous "closes" acting as ribs. A close, or wynd, is a narrow alley branching off the Royal Mile to the north and south. Many of these closes run steeply downhill, prompting builders to construct tall tenements, possibly creating the world's first skyscrapers, some up to fourteen storeys high. Some closes were early examples of gated communities, as their narrowness made them easy to secure and keep troublemakers out. At one time, there were around 248 closes. Our next story takes place just off one of these closes, in Chessel's Court, which has links to a literary classic and its own intriguing history.

William Brodie (1741–88), a prominent figure in Edinburgh's society, held esteemed positions as a skilled cabinet-maker and a respected member of the town council, serving as deacon of the Incorporation of Wrights and Masons. However, unbeknownst to the upper echelons of society,

Brodie led a clandestine double life as the ringleader of a band of burglars. This nocturnal pursuit was necessitated by his extravagant lifestyle, which included multiple mistresses, numerous offspring, and a penchant for gambling.

Brodie's day job provided the perfect cover for his illicit activities, involving the crafting and repairing of security locks and mechanisms. Succumbing to temptation, he secretly copied his trusting clients' keys while working on their locks, enabling him and his three cohorts – Brown, Smith, and Ainslie – to carry out robberies at their leisure.

The pinnacle of Brodie's criminal career and subsequent downfall came with an armed raid on His Majesty's Excise Office in Chessel's Court. Although Brodie masterminded the burglary, it ended disastrously when Ainslie and Brown were apprehended and turned informants. Brodie fled to the Netherlands but was later captured in Amsterdam and extradited to Edinburgh for trial.

Despite a lack of substantial evidence, a search of Brodie's residence uncovered incriminating tools of his trade. He and Smith were convicted, and their execution was scheduled for 1 October 1788. Brodie met his demise at the Tolbooth alongside his accomplice George Smith despite attempting to cheat the noose by wearing a steel collar. His execution took place on a gallows he had recently redesigned, a macabre twist of fate that underscored the irony of his demise. Brodie was laid to rest in an unmarked grave at the Parish Church in Buccleuch.

Brodie's enigmatic double life served as inspiration for Robert Louis Stevenson, who incorporated elements of his story into the classic tale of split personality *The Strange Case of Dr. Jekyll and Mr. Hyde*. Stevenson's connection to Brodie through his father, who commissioned furniture from him, further solidified the link between reality and fiction.

Today, Chessel's Court, built by the eighteenth-century merchant and property developer Archibald Chessel, stands as a reminder of Edinburgh's intriguing past, with tales of deception and intrigue etched into its very walls.

As the supernatural story unfolds, our attention shifts to a Mrs Gordon, a wealthy resident of Chessel's Court, whose dwelling is shrouded in unsettling tales of the "Lady in Black". The origins of this haunting are not fully known but are believed to have started sometime in the eighteenth century.

It began subtly enough for Mrs Gordon, who lived alone, to initially dismiss it.

Amid a biting, inky winter night, she settled down to read by the warmth of her fire, the dim light of her candle casting flickering shadows on the walls but providing enough light for her to make out the words on the pages of her favourite book. With Chessel's Court set back from the busy Royal Mile, there was little noise to disturb her. The only sounds breaking the silence were the ticking of her clock and the crackling of the fire.

Engrossed in her book, she gradually became aware of something amiss. Her attention was drawn to the front door of her home. She listened intently and heard a noise outside – something indistinct at first. Curious, she put down her book and approached the locked door, pressing her ear against the wood.

She heard heavy breathing on the other side, as if someone had climbed the steep steps to her house and stopped to catch their breath, or ponder their next action. After a minute or two, the breathing stopped, and the welcome silence of the night returned.

Although she lived in an affluent area of Edinburgh, residing at the top of a steep staircase in an overcrowded city, she reasoned that the heavy breathing could be from anyone – a neighbour, a drunk, or perhaps even an animal – so she paid little heed to it. But this was the first night of many when she would hear this unnerving sound.

Several nights passed before she heard the laboured breathing again; indeed enough time had passed that she'd almost forgotten what had happened previously. When she heard the breathing outside her property again, she mustered the courage to investigate. Pulling open the heavy front door, Mrs Gordon saw no one. She stepped outside for a better look, using a candle to illuminate the stairs, but again, no one. She saw only the darkness of the night, with a distant street lamp casting long shadows across the silent close. There was nothing and no one to be seen.

Over time, Mrs Gordon grew accustomed to her breathless visitor, who had never revealed themselves, only making their presence known through the laboured breathing she often heard. However, soon enough, others would come to experience it too, not just Mrs Gordon.

The source of the breathing was revealed when Mrs Gordon's brother spent the night in her main room. A peaceful evening had passed, and to her relief, there had been no sign of the nocturnal visitor outside her door. Mrs Gordon feared her brother would think she had lost her mind had she told him about her experiences, but he would soon find out about the haunting for himself.

After retiring for the evening and falling soundly asleep, Mr Gordon was awoken in the "wee sma' hours" by an unmistakable sense that he was not alone. As his eyes adjusted to the dark, he fumbled for a candle and some matches, straining to see what had disturbed his sleep.

He eventually struck a match, and to his horror, the light revealed the apparition of a tall, veiled woman. She stood before him, dressed head to toe in black, gliding out of a recess and across the room. Her presence was silent and her gaze indifferent, yet she was as solid as you or me. Then, just as quickly as she appeared, she vanished, and Mr Gordon's match went out. It was said that he "nearly lost his mind" and fled the house in panic without seeing out the night, never to return.

This wasn't the end of the haunting of Chessel's Court. The veiled woman has been encountered in modern times, her presence still felt in the old house and the impressive courtyard.

In 1985, a tenant lodged in number four Chessel's Court spoke of a terrifying encounter:

> "One night, I had been asleep but had woken and got up tae get myself a drink of water; this was about 1.30am.
>
> "After climbing back in tae bed, I heard my landlady's dog growling and scratching at my door to get in.
>
> "At that same moment, something or someone came through the wall beside my bed and started to climb over me. I could feel it pushing down on the blankets as it climbed over me.
>
> "This went on for what seemed like forever, but would say was about two minutes, with the dog growling at the door all the time.

> "It was pitch dark. I just froze and would nae move. While lying there, I was thinking if I sat up fast, what would happen? Would I be face tae face with something that I could nae see, as it was so dark, or will it just go through me? Something I did nae want tae happen fae sure.
>
> "As soon as it got to the other side of my bed and climbed off me, the dog stopped growling and went back to her bed.
>
> "I waited a few moments, then got up, turned the light on and looked about the room and out the window, but there was nothing to be found.
>
> "The next day, I told my landlady what had happened, and she said she never heard a thing. I found that strange in itself, as the dog used tae sleep just outside her room, and every other time at night when the dog had got up fae whatever reason, she always woke, but not this time!"

John Tantallon, from the fantastic North Edinburgh Nightmares, contacted me in 2023 about a creepy encounter that happened to him while staying in Chessel's Court, which could be proof that the Lady in Black still haunts Chessel's court.

John writes:

> "In October of 2016, the same night that John Carpenter played the Usher Hall, we had friends over from America, and they asked us to hire them accommodation for a week.
>
> "We got a holiday flat above the Canons' Gait pub. The group wouldn't arrive until Saturday, so me and my ex, Vicky, decided to stay in it on the Friday night.
>
> "Vicky was hungry and ordered a pizza from somewhere nearby to be delivered. Over the next half hour, she heard

> three or four instances of someone in the stair and, each time, presuming it to be the delivery, answered the door. There was nobody there at any time.
>
> "When the pizza did arrive, the sound of footsteps was entirely different to anything she'd heard in the last half hour; you could hear every noise clear as day.
>
> "There was nobody else in any of the flats in the stair, as it was out of season.
>
> "A spooky evening, make no mistake..."

With its phantom footsteps, disembodied breathing, and chilling apparitions of a woman in black, for me, this story contains all the classic elements of a ghostly encounter. John's firsthand experiences and the unsettling encounter in 1985 attest to the ongoing nature of these occurrences, underscoring the significance of including this story in our collection.

What makes this story so compelling is its almost forgotten nature. Despite its rich mosaic of haunting elements, it has faded into obscurity over the years. As a boy, I was captivated by the famous novel *The Woman in Black,* which brought to life the haunting presence of a spectral figure shrouded in mystery. This tale of Chessel's Court similarly captured my imagination, evoking the same chills and fascination that Susan Hill's novel did. The ghostly woman in black, who haunts the old house and its impressive courtyard, mirrors the timeless appeal of Hill's creation, adding another layer of intrigue and resonance to this Edinburgh legend.

This tale deserves to be remembered and shared, highlighting the eerie and mysterious charm that continues to define Edinburgh. The encounters at Chessel's Court offer a unique glimpse into the lingering spectre of Deacon Brodie's deeds, echoing through the centuries in the form of inexplicable phenomena. While the story may dwell in the shadows of Edinburgh's history, its resonance persists, drawing parallels between the real and the supernatural, deepening the city's rich history of folklore and legend.

CHAPTER 3
THE CANONGATE

Contrary to popular belief, the famous Royal Mile isn't as old as first imagined. The name "Royal Mile" is very much a twentieth-century construct, and while the route is ancient, the name isn't. Its first recorded use was by W. M. Gilbert in 1901 in his book *Edinburgh in the Nineteenth Century.*

The Royal Mile – an ancient Scots mile measuring 1.81 kilometres – winds its way from Edinburgh Castle down to the palace of Holyrood House. Contrary to its name, it's not a single continuous street but a series of interconnected thoroughfares, including the Lawnmarket, the High Street, Castlehill, and the Canongate – the setting of our story today.

The origins of the Canongate stretch back to the eleventh century when monks from Holyrood Abbey established a burgh in the area. The term "Canongate", derived from Scots, translates to "Canon's Way". This was the path the canons, or members of the clergy, would traverse from Holyrood to the castle.

During the turbulent years of the Jacobite rebellions, the streets of the Canongate bore witness to the ebb and flow of political unrest that swept through Scotland. As Jacobite supporters rallied behind their cause, the Canongate became a thoroughfare for their aspirations and struggles. Royal proclamations echoed through its cobbled lanes, rallying cries resounded from its taverns, and the tramp of marching feet reverberated off its storied walls.

In 1745, during the height of the Jacobite uprising, Bonnie Prince Charlie, the charismatic leader of the Jacobite forces, made his triumphant entry into Edinburgh via the Canongate. Amidst fervent cheers and waving banners, he traversed the historic streets, buoyed by the support of his followers, who eagerly awaited the restoration of the Stuart monarchy.

Yet the Canongate also bore witness to the darker side of rebellion. Government troops, loyal to the Hanoverian crown, marched through its thoroughfares in pursuit of Jacobite insurgents. The clash of arms and the cries of battle echoed through its streets as the fate of nations hung in the balance.

In the aftermath of the Jacobite defeat at the Battle of Culloden in 1746, the Canongate witnessed the sombre procession of defeated rebels as they were brought to justice. The once jubilant streets now stood silent, bearing witness to the heavy toll of conflict and the end of Jacobite dreams.

Nestled within the Canongate is an area referred to as "Bible Land", also known as "Shoemakers Land" due to its former inhabitants, cobblers. Above numbers 185 and 187, there's a distinctive stone carving that lends the building its "Bible Land" moniker. This carving bears an excerpt from Psalm 133: "Behold how good a thing it is and how becoming well, Together such as brethren are in unity to dwell."

It was here, likely in the seventeenth or eighteenth centuries, that a murder is said to have taken place, the murder of an anonymous woman now only known for wearing a tartan dress and white apron and, importantly for us, haunting the location.

The woman was said to have been murdered on the landing of one of the top-floor flats in Bible Land, stabbed to death by an unknown murderer. It wasn't long after her restless spirit started to haunt the residents of Bible Land.

It's widely believed that sudden, violent acts like this, where there is an immediate release of energy, get trapped in the surrounding stone, and later, when the conditions are right, the event is somehow replayed. This is more commonly known as the "stone tape theory". Given how frequent her apparition was at first, this must have been a truly shocking and sudden act if this theory is to be believed.

Oddly, the people of the stair (the block of flats) soon became familiar with the phantom, and seeing her just became as commonplace as seeing your neighbour – that is, for everyone except a gentleman named Mr Scrougal.

One late evening, Mr Scrougal returned home from a romantic outing with his sweetheart, a skip in his step and thoughts of their pleasant evening lingering in his mind. As he ascended the stairs to his flat, his heart still buoyed by the affectionate moments shared, he was suddenly confronted by a chilling sight upon reaching the top landing. There, standing before him, was the ghostly apparition of the tartan-clad murder victim.

Shock and terror seized him in that moment, causing him to recoil instinctively, his body tensing as he teetered dangerously close to the edge of the staircase. The fear that gripped him was so profound that it threatened to send him tumbling backward down the stairs in his haste to escape the spectral presence.

For several days, Mr Scrougal kept the harrowing encounter to himself, wary of the potential ridicule and disbelief he might face from others. Sadly, his apprehensions proved justified when he finally mustered the courage to share his tale. Instead of receiving sympathy or understanding, he was met with scorn and mockery from the locals, who dismissed his experience as an exaggeration or a flight of fancy.

In particular, the father of his sweetheart, perhaps seeking to assert his authority or simply revelling in the opportunity to belittle Mr Scrougal, subjected him to relentless taunting and jests. The ridicule became unbearable, straining the relationship between Mr Scrougal and his sweetheart to the breaking point. In the end, he chose to sever ties with her family, seeking solace and companionship elsewhere.

As Mr Scrougal embarked on a new chapter in his life, finding love anew with another, one can't help but wonder if he ever shared the tale of his haunting encounter with his new paramour. Perhaps he kept it tucked away, a secret reminder of the inexplicable and unsettling events that can occur in the shadows of everyday life.

There's a haunting truth that has always lingered in my thoughts: the notion that within just three generations, one can be forgotten by their own family. In today's digital age, where countless selfies and family photos are snapped and shared, this idea may seem outdated. However, a closer look at history reveals that this phenomenon is not as distant as we might imagine.

In the case of the Bible Land apparition, this notion of forgotten identity hits particularly hard. It's a tragedy that we've lost the name and the story of the victim of such a horrendous crime. Who was she? Why was she murdered? These questions remain unanswered, buried beneath the sands of time.

By including her story in this book, I hope to preserve at least a fragment of her memory, to ensure that she is not consigned to the shadows of forgotten history. In death, as in life, every individual deserves to be remembered, their identity preserved for future generations to acknowledge and honour.

CHAPTER 4
THE MUSEUM OF EDINBURGH

In addition to its numerous castles, copious pubs, and an incredible number of ghosts, Edinburgh is also home to many world-famous museums. Perhaps the best known and most renowned is the Royal Museum of Scotland, which dominates Chambers Street in the heart of the city.

Founded in 1854, the Royal Museum traces its origins to the amalgamation of various collections, including those of the Society of Antiquaries of Scotland and the Board of Manufactures. Over the years, the museum has undergone several expansions and renovations, evolving into the magnificent institution it is today. With its diverse array of exhibits spanning natural history, world cultures, science, and technology, the Royal Museum of Scotland offers visitors a comprehensive journey through the realms of knowledge. From ancient artefacts to cutting-edge scientific discoveries, the museum's collections continue to inspire curiosity and awe, making it a beloved destination for locals and tourists alike.

However, if you want a more authentic experience focused solely on Edinburgh, then continue down the Royal Mile and you'll discover the wonderful, historic Museum of Edinburgh.

The Museum of Edinburgh offers a fantastic, immersive journey through the history and culture of Scotland's capital. It features artefacts, exhibits, and interactive displays that showcase Edinburgh's incredible heritage, from its earliest origins to more recent times. The museum consists of several buildings that have been interconnected over the years to create the museum complex. These buildings include Huntly House, which serves as the main entrance and houses many of the museum's displays and exhibits. Huntly House is one of the oldest buildings in the Old Town and a historic mansion that has played a significant role in the city's history. The house is named after George Gordon, the 1st Marquess of Huntly, the owner of the property in the sixteenth century.

Huntly was a powerful Scottish nobleman and played an important role in the political and social affairs of the time. His early life was marked by the turbulent political and religious changes of the era, including the Protestant Reformation. He grew up during a time of shifting alliances and conflicts among clans and families, and his political allegiances were complex, often aligning with the interests of the Scottish crown. He served as a loyal supporter of King James VI of Scotland, but his political manoeuvring sometimes placed him at odds with other noble families – most notably the Clan Campbell.

In 2023, I had the privilege of speaking with someone who shared firsthand encounters during her time working at the museum.

As someone intimately familiar with the inner workings and the creepy occurrences that unfold when darkness descends, she brings us a unique perspective on the stories we don't often get to hear about.

She told me:

> "I was mostly based in the Museum of Edinburgh, where I would do what I called the 'occasional tour'.
>
> "On my very first day there, I was told there was the ghost of a female who was described as tall, blonde and with curly hair. She was seen wearing a white period dress with black details, on the top floor in the Edinburgh crystal display room. Given I was the new girl on the block, I assumed my colleagues were obviously trying to scare me, but it failed, so I spent most of the day in that room but nothing. Just in case though, I always used to say, 'Good morning, m'lady,' every time I opened up that room.
>
> "For years, I waited to see if this woman would appear to me, but I had no hint of a sighting.
>
> "However, on my very last day, I was doing my patrol, and from the corner of my eye, I saw a figure standing to my side. I turned my head to look, and I saw this tall lady with blonde curly hair, wearing a white period dress with black details on it – just as the ghost was described. The woman was looking out the window towards the Royal Mile, apparently lost in her thoughts. After a second or two, she turned towards me and...smiled...then disappeared.
>
> "I couldn't believe it. I'd waited eight years to see her, and I saw her on my last day working there.
>
> "I never felt scared or worried in that room, but the next room held a lot of exhibits that once belonged to Field Marshal Earl Haigh, and was a completely different story."

Acheson House, now part of the Museum of Edinburgh, is a historic mansion with a fascinating history dating back to the seventeenth century. Sir Archibald Acheson (c. 1580–1634) was a Scottish lawyer who moved to Ireland in 1610, but maintained his position in Scotland. He served as a member of the Parliament of Scotland in 1625 and was appointed a Lord of Session in 1627. Before 1634, he held the office of Secretary of State for Scotland under Charles I.

Sir Archibald and his wife, Margaret Hamilton, built Acheson House in 1633, though he might never have lived there, as he died the following year. In 1636, the house was sold to Edinburgh merchant Patrick Wood and subsequently passed through many owners, including the Incorporation of Bakers in 1784. The house was subdivided in the eighteenth century and became a brothel by the early nineteenth century. From 1830 to 1924, it was owned by the Slater family.

In the twentieth century, declining living standards in the Old Town led to widespread slum clearance. Acheson House was bought by the city council, but the 4th Marquess of Bute, an antiquarian, purchased it in 1935. He commissioned architect Robert Hurd to carry out a restoration. In 1938, it was proposed that the house become the official residence of the Secretary of State for Scotland, but in 1939, it was acquired by the Canongate Kirk and used by the Iona Community, an ecumenical group. Between 1947 and 1951, an educational book publisher and his family lived there. From 1951, it became the Scottish Craft Centre, showcasing contemporary Scottish craftwork until its closure in 1991. The building remained empty for twenty years and was added to the Buildings at Risk Register for Scotland in 2000. By 2007, plans were made to incorporate it into the Museum of Edinburgh. In 2011, the house was renovated, and in November of that year, the Edinburgh World Heritage Trust moved into the building from its previous base at 5 Charlotte Square.

The house is a fine example of the Scottish Renaissance architectural style, characterised by its intricate stone carvings, ornate façade, and distinctive crow-stepped gables.

One of the most notable aspects of Acheson House is its connection to the writer Sir Walter Scott. In the nineteenth century, Scott was a friend of the Bute family and spent time in Acheson House. It's said that he used the house as a model for the home of Jonathan Oldbuck, a character in his novel *The Antiquary.*

Linzi discovered that history wasn't the only thing lingering within the walls of Acheson House – ghostly tales awaited her as well:

> "In 2011, they were doing renovation work to join Acheson House with Huntly House and convert some of the property into the offices for Edinburgh World Heritage. We know that renovation work can stir up stuff, and holy shit, did it ever!
>
> "All of a sudden, the odd noise or footsteps became ghost children standing in the corner, singing, giggling, or following you about. Every day I see someone. I'm sensitive to spirit and a bit of an empath, so I was really badly affected during these times and could not get any peace.
>
> "One day, it was my turn to open up at 7am for the workmen. I went in the front door of Acheson House, totally feeling like someone was present, but I tried to shrug the feeling and continued to switch the alarm off. On my way out, I glance to the doorway and see this tall shadow figure lunge at me, and I swear to god, I've never run so fast in my

life! Normally, I'm pretty level-headed these days, but I don't know if something in my head was saying, 'Run!'

"I wasn't 100% sure if maybe someone had broken in or followed me in, as there were homeless people who would sleep in the Canongate Kirk. My original thought was, 'Oh my god, is this a real person?!' but no one ran out, and luckily for me at the same time I'm running out of the building, my boss arrived. I told her what I'd experienced, so we both agreed it was best to check the building together – safety in numbers as they say. We stuck together and moved through the building room by room, but no one was there. It was empty.

"After that she told me, 'You aren't doing early mornings. I don't care what the others say, the ghosts are scaring you.' The whole renovation project was crazy active. The poor painters and decorators even had stuff happen to them while they worked, like hearing children giggling.

"The staff generally got on well, but I dunno, sometimes there would be petty arguments between people for no reason, which I found odd, as we all worked together for years and got on well together despite some long boring days.

"I know I was heavily affected. I found it extremely draining at times. I soon earned a new name due to my experiences, and the workmen started calling me 'ghost girl'.

"The scariest one was in the early hours of the morning at about 3am. That night, the fire alarm went off, and three fire engines, the fire chief, and the call-out guy showed up, but there was nothing on fire – it seemed like it was just a false alarm. When they inspected further, what they did find was that the 'break glass' panel had been smashed for no reason.

> Nothing had fallen and hit it, and the cold wouldn't affect it in this way. We did ask, but the firemen were stumped and made a joke about us maybe having a ghost…completely unaware of the activities.
>
> "As for the atmosphere in the place, a few sceptical people would start to feel uneasy, and some of them actually experienced footsteps running away from them from the locked gates. Even the poor ADT alarm guys hated going around the building on their own, which, I'll be honest, I found a little funny."

I have been to the Museum of Edinburgh several times. I first visited by accident when I was walking up the Royal Mile with my kids and confused the museum with the Museum of Childhood, which is a couple of minutes further up the road.

I had no expectations when I went in, but came out feeling I knew next to nothing about the city I have lived in for most of my life, so quickly arranged another visit. I can't say I've ever felt uncomfortable there or noticed a presence, but my visits are short and usually when the museum has many other visitors walking its rooms, so my attention is elsewhere. That's why I was immediately taken with Linzi's experiences.

She is in these historic buildings when others are not, a solitary presence amidst empty rooms and quiet streets, where only memories remain. It's as though the echoes of the past still reverberate through the ancient walls, carrying whispers of bygone eras and forgotten souls.

Is it any wonder that these buildings, steeped in the city's history and haunted by the lingering spirits of some of its former residents, seem to hold secrets untold? If you subscribe to the "Stone Tape" theory, which posits that emotional or traumatic events can be "recorded" onto the environment and replayed under certain conditions, could this explain the inexplicable occurrences that seem to defy rational explanation?

Would this explain the disembodied children's laughter, or could this be down to their spirits being grounded in the properties, refusing – or being unable – to leave their last moments of joy and innocence behind? Whatever the case, these ghostly reverberations serve as a reminder that the past is never truly gone, and that the spirits of those who once walked these halls may still linger among us, their presence felt but their stories untold.

Unreported stories like Linzi's are the main reason behind me starting Eerie Edinburgh. With the focus on the more "marketable" locations previously mentioned, we are in danger of becoming oblivious to some of the more subtle yet equally intriguing stories that deserve to be told. It's essential that we not only uncover these hidden tales but also preserve them for the future, ensuring that the rich mosaic of Edinburgh's supernatural history remains intact.

Thank you to Linzi for sharing her story.

CHAPTER 5
QUEENSBERRY HOUSE

Near the foot of the Royal Mile, opposite Holyrood Palace, stands the modern Scottish Parliament building. Built after the devolution referendum in 1997 and officially opened in 2004, the building is now a space for democratic discussions and debates that shape the future of modern-day Scotland. Further up the Mile, there is Parliament House. A grand and imposing building situated in the heart of Edinburgh's historic Old Town. Parliament House is a prominent symbol of Scotland's legal and political history and, until the early eighteenth century, the site of the old Parliament of Scotland. Originally constructed in 1639, and the world's first purpose-built parliament, this magnificent edifice has witnessed centuries of political debates, legal proceedings, and significant events that have shaped the nation. It was here in 1706 that the Treaty of Union was signed by a group of English and Scottish commissioners nominated by Queen Anne, the then monarch, with guidance from the Duke of Argyll and James Douglas, the second Duke of Queensberry.

The Douglas family lived in a grand house in the Canongate called Queensberry House, which still stands to this day. Queensberry House holds a fascinating and storied past that dates back to the seventeenth century. Built around 1680, it was originally for Lord Hatton, as master of the Scottish mint. Ownership transferred over to William Douglas, the first Duke of Queensberry, a prominent figure in Scottish politics during the Restoration period, when he bought the house in 1686. William's death would be the first death in the house in 1695, and after this, ownership of Queensberry House passed to his son James, the second Duke of Queensberry. Two years later in 1697, Douglas had a son also called James, but young James would go on to earn a far less distinguished title.

From an early age, it became clear that young James wouldn't live a traditional life. He was prone to fits of anger and violent outbursts. He'd attack those charged with raising him and punch or bite children he should have been playing with. His reputation, earned at such a young age, led him to be described by some who knew him or witnessed his behaviour as "an imbecile" and "violently insane".

Due to his nature and the sensibilities of the day, the Douglases took a drastic course of action: they locked him away in a room that had only one way in or one way out. And the key to that room was held only by his father. The only human interaction young James had in the years he was locked up was when he was given his daily food or held down so he could be cleaned and changed. This drastic and seemingly inhumane act was taken as a safety precaution – not for James, but for the others who lived in the house.

In 1707, when James was ten, the Treaty of Union was signed. The Treaty of Union united the Kingdom of Scotland and the

Kingdom of England into a single sovereign state known as the Kingdom of Great Britain.

On the day of signing, there was a mixture of celebration and rioting. The union was unpopular among ordinary people, as Rabbie Burns so eloquently put it, "We're bought and sold, for English gold. Such a parcel of rogues, in a nation." But for those who would prosper, the Union brought opportunity and the promise of riches. The Duke of Queensberry was among this group, and he and his family are believed to have left Queensberry House to join in the celebrations or to escape while the city rioted. During this time, only a kitchen boy was left in the house along with young James.

No one knows how – perhaps it happened during the rush to celebrate or the panic to escape – but somehow James's door was left unlocked and unguarded. A few hours passed before the Duke, his family, and the rest of the servants returned, tired and hungry. Stepping into the grand home, they were met with the unmistakably pleasant smell of a roaring fire and assumed a meal was being prepared. While the family retreated to their private quarters, one servant followed the smell and walked down the twisting stone staircase towards the kitchen to see what was being cooked.

None of the usual candles had been lit in the dark and gloomy room; the only light was coming from the large open fire used to cook. The flames cast shadows that danced along the stone walls. As they stood at the entrance to the kitchen, the servant could see the silhouette of a small figure with their back to them sat to the side of the fire, working the spit. Assuming it was the kitchen boy, they called out to him and asked what was being prepared, but received no answer. They called again: still no answer. Frustrated by this perceived insolence, they approached the boy and tapped him on the shoulder. The face that met them when he turned round was not that of the kitchen help, but that of young James, who had escaped his confinement. It was then the servant's horrified gaze fell upon what was being cooked on the spit – the body of the poor, unfortunate kitchen boy.

A horrendous scream shattered the silence and echoed around the halls of the lofty mansion. Everyone in the house heard it and immediately rushed to the kitchen to investigate. While they ran to the kitchen, the servant who'd discovered this macabre scene ran in the opposite direction out into the street, screaming as they went. The Duke's reaction was just as horrified. His young son had killed, cooked, and eaten a servant in his charge. The young boy's blood was splattered on the walls around the fireplace and smeared over the grinning mouth of his own flesh and blood. Young James was immediately apprehended and confined to his room, and the remains of the poor kitchen boy were solemnly removed from the spit.

The aftermath of this story is almost as horrific as the act itself. The power and position the Duke held meant no criminal charges were brought against his murderous son. Other than some critics of the Treaty of Union, who claimed it a "judgement on the Duke for his odious share in the Union", it was almost as if the abhorrent event hadn't happened. In fact, his heir was allowed to inherit the Marquisate and Earldom of Queensberry but, due to his mental state, did not succeed to the Dukedom.

Although young James passed away in 1715, the harrowing impact of this tragic event continues to reverberate through the ages. Frequently, the air around the fireplace is filled with eerie and terrified screams, haunting the space with their inexplicable origin. Many witnesses have described these bone-chilling cries as the anguished voice of a young boy, forever etched into the haunted history of the place.

From the early 1800s until 1996, Queensberry House was used as a hospital or home for the elderly. Throughout this time, chilling reports emerged of shadowy forms seen darting about the cold and draughty corridors, and blood-curdling screams have been seemingly unrelated to any of the patients' voices. Some nursing staff even spoke of being pinned against walls in one particular area by an unseen force. Perhaps this was where James grabbed the unsuspecting kitchen boy before slaughtering him? In an ironic turn of events in 1997, Queensberry House, once owned by a man in part responsible for the dissolution of the old parliament, was acquired by the newly formed Parliament and is now used as office space for administrative staff.

While the past horrors of the kitchen boy's tragic fate may still echo within the walls, the area where the oven still stands has undergone a modern refurbishment, transforming into an exclusive private bar for MPs and their guests. One can't help but wonder, as they raise their glasses in a toast, are these the only spirits that remain in Queensberry House?

When I thought about putting together this book, one story immediately came to mind as essential: the chilling account of the cannibal in Edinburgh. It's a personal favourite of mine, told to me by an uncle when I was a young boy. I am fascinated by this story both for its intriguing nature and its spooky undertone, and it's a building I'd love to explore further. The notion of a cannibal's ghost lingering in the house where he was once imprisoned, especially considering his noble lineage, contrasts with Scotland's more well-known cannibal, Sawney Bean, making it a compelling inclusion.

Given the fascination with the darker aspects of ghost stories and ghost hunting, it's surprising that this particular tale has been inexplicably overlooked, it's possible that it's because the building is inaccessible due to its current purpose, but it could also be down to being such an uncomfortable subject matter.

In my opinion, it's a story like no other, with origins uniquely rooted in Edinburgh and deserving of inclusion.

CHAPTER 6
HOLYROOD PALACE

Towards the end of the Royal Mile, a few hundred feet from Queensberry House, Holyrood Abbey stands as a silent, regal witness to nearly a thousand years of Scotland's tumultuous and incredible history.

Holyrood's origins date to the heart of the mediaeval period, when King David I of Scotland established Holyrood Abbey in 1128 as a sanctuary for Augustinian monks. Legend ties its founding to a pivotal event: during the Feast of the Cross in 1127, King David I ventured into the dense forests east of Edinburgh. There, amidst the wilderness, he had an extraordinary encounter that would shape the site's future, embedding its story deeply within Scottish history.

Separated from his hunting party, the King rode alone through the forest, surrounded by towering trees. Yet danger lurked nearby. Suddenly, a large stag emerged from the undergrowth and charged towards him. The King was thrown from his horse in the ensuing chaos. As he faced the furious stag on the forest floor, a moment of intense struggle ensued between man and beast. However, just when it seemed all hope was lost, a divine light appeared between the stag's antlers, startling the creature and causing it to flee. This unexpected turn of events saved the King from harm, marking an encounter that would become a part of Scottish folklore for generations to come.

As a gesture of gratitude for what was perceived as a miraculous event, King David built Holyrood Abbey the following year. The abbey took its name from the "Haly Ruid" (Holy Cross), as it was believed to house a fragment of the true cross in a golden reliquary. This religious foundation swiftly became a prominent centre of worship and education throughout the mediaeval period.

Constructed in both Romanesque and Gothic architectural styles, Holyrood Abbey held profound spiritual significance for centuries. Pilgrims journeyed here seeking blessings and spiritual solace, drawn by the abbey's sacred relics and its association with King David's legendary encounter. It also served as a place of sanctuary for those in need. A protective aura encompassed the abbey, extending for five miles to include substantial portions of the adjacent Holyrood Park.

Within this expanse of sanctuary, debtors sought refuge and reprieve, turning to the esteemed Bailie of Holyroodhouse as their beacon of hope. Now marked out by brass sanctuary stones, the outline of this area where many sought refuge can be traced along the Royal Mile. Those deemed deserving of its shield became more than just beneficiaries; they were christened "Abbey Lairds". With this honour, they not only found sanctuary but also discovered solace within the walls of the abbey, where they were embraced by shelter and support. This enduring bond secured their place in history, ensuring that their legacy would be remembered for generations to come.

Adjacent to the abbey, Holyrood Palace's origins trace back to the late 1600s when King James IV, envisioning a magnificent residence, gave it life.

His aim was clear: a grand palace fit for Scottish monarchs during their visits to Edinburgh, providing a place where both royal life and state affairs could seamlessly coexist. The finished palace is exactly that, a palace fit for royalty with 294 separate rooms serving various functions, including state apartments, private apartments, and exhibition spaces.

This unique blend of the sacred and the regal is how Holyroodhouse earned its name, intertwining its religious heritage with its monarchical role.

Throughout the ages, Holyrood Palace became the site of a multitude of momentous historical events, and its halls hosted an array of prominent historical figures, many who helped shape Scotland as we know it.

Against this backdrop, you might find it unsurprising that some of them chose to linger beyond their time, and their spirits still remain in the hallowed halls of Haunted Holyrood. Perhaps the most famous, or infamous, event to take place in the palace is the brutal murder of David Rizzio.

Rizzio was an Italian courtier and the private secretary of Mary, Queen of Scots and close friend of the Queen.

Their relationship was so intimate that it gave rise to whispers and rumours among the nobility of the time. It was even said that her unborn son, the future King James the 6th, was a product of their hidden relationship. Eventually and unsurprisingly, these rumours made their way to Mary's husband, Lord Darnley: jealousy took hold, and a plot was hatched.

On the night of 9 March 1566, Darnley and his supporters overpowered the Royal Guard and burst into the Queen's chamber, demanding the Queen hand over Rizzio – to which she refused.

It's said that one of the attackers, Patrick Bellenden, even threatened the life of the unborn future king by pointing his loaded pistol at the Queen's pregnant belly.

A further struggle ensued, and Rizzio was forcibly dragged from the bedchamber into the adjoining Audience Chamber, where he met a gruesome end by being stabbed a reported fifty-seven times.

His lifeless body was callously discarded down the main staircase, and his life's treasures, including precious jewels and fine attire, were callously stripped from his corpse.

Death wouldn't be the end of Rizzio however, and his ghostly apparition was soon seen regularly in the area where he spent his last terrifying moments.

As the story goes, Rizzio's ghost is said to appear in the palace, often in the presence of women. His ghostly figure is described as distressed and appears as if seeking protection or assistance. It's suggested that his spirit remains restless due to the violent and brutal nature of his murder and the betrayal he suffered at the hands of those he served.

Towards the end of the 1970s, author of the 1987 book *Haunted Royal Homes,* Joan Forman, stayed in the palace to research the many stories associated with Holyrood, for her chapter on the palace. She wrote of one room:

> "I found it quite impossible to stay in this, the small supper or supping room for more than a few minutes at a time, and matters were made worse by the fact that the sense of horror

> which afflicts it appears to be concentrated in one single area, the left hand side near the entrance door. The sensation is so intense that it almost seems to have weight – as though the very air was thicker at that spot."

The room the author referred to is the room in which Rizzio met his murderous end.

There is a bloodstain on the site of the murder, often referred to as "Rizzio's bloodstain". Over the years, there have been several attempts to remove the stain, but the efforts have been in vain, as no matter how hard it's scrubbed, the stain remains. The floorboards have even been replaced, but the stain is said to soon reappear.

In 1896, Holyrood welcomed one of the Victorian era's most notable psychical researchers: Frederic Myers. He had travelled to the palace to interview the wife of the palace's Lord High Commissioner, Lady Tweedale, about her experiences while living in Holyrood.

From an early age, Lady Tweedale had numerous experiences that led her to believe there was life after death, but an experience one night in the palace is one that stayed with her more than most.

On retiring for the night, rather than sleeping, she was sitting upright in her heavy iron-framed bed, reading.

Alone and enthralled in her book, she felt relaxed and comfortable until the heavy bed was pushed out from the wall – "pulled violently", as she described it.

After the initial excitement, silence returned to the room, and Lady Tweedale looked around for the agent that caused the movement. As she was doing this, the bed moved again. She is quoted as saying, "I jumped up and saw that it had actually been moved – perhaps about a foot – so that there was a clear space between the head of the bed and wall there had not been before."

After this second seemingly supernatural movement, activity ceased, and Lady Tweedale was able to rest for the remainder of the evening.

That was until the following night when the same thing happened again, with no rational cause.

Due to the ongoing activity, Lady Tweedale refused to be alone in the room, and this action seemed to put an end to that particular activity, and she was never troubled by the movement again.

In the same year, Lady Tweedale reported an even stranger encounter.

This time it wasn't poltergeist-type phenomena that terrified her, this time the event that made her blood run cold was when she saw a spectre appear. A lavish reception was held one evening, one attended by close to one thousand people. As the evening wore on and guests started to make their way home, Lady Tweedale, exhausted by her hostess duties, took a seat in a nook in what's called the Throne Room.

Across from where she rested was a large, heavy door that hadn't been opened for some time and was very securely fastened shut.

From her position, she could still see the band, who continued to play. She allowed herself a few minutes of peace where she could listen to the music and enjoy watching the remaining couples dance.

Her attention was soon drawn back to the door, once securely fastened, now wide open.

Emerging from the darkness she could see a figure walking towards her, a figure she described as male, tall, dark, and handsome, dressed in all black and wearing what she took to be a military coat from the period of Charles the 2nd.

The figure continued his determined march past her and into the room as the band played – astonishingly walking through them as they continued to play without disturbance – before disappearing through a centre window that looked out to the courtyard fifteen feet below.

After the figure disappeared, Lady Tweedale ran to the bandmaster and asked if he had seen the mysterious visitor before he vanished. "No," was his reply, "but I felt a draft from the door." The bandmaster was referring to the door from which the figure first appeared – now fastened once again.

Although attempts were made to try to identify the figure she had witnessed – at one point she felt it may have been Mary, Queen of Scot's husband the Earl of Bothwell – no one was ever conclusively identified as being the spectre, and his identity remains as much a mystery as his one and only appearance was.

As you can imagine, given the substantial count of 294 rooms, the palace boasts an even greater number of windows, all of which require regular cleaning.

This is the kind of prestigious and lucrative contract local window cleaners would fall over themselves to win, and the windows of one area of the palace would play an integral part of another notable haunting.

The Long Gallery in Holyrood Palace is a regal and historically significant space adorned with portraits of monarchs and historical figures. Decorated with ornate furnishings, the area was reportedly widely used and favoured by Mary, Queen of Scots.

In the late 1970s, numerous stories of disembodied footsteps were often reported, slowly and deliberately making their way along the length of this stately room.

In late autumn 1977, a window cleaner was working in the room and cleaning an area near the top of an open window.

In true horror-movie style, the window was half open, and as they moved it, they were shocked to see reflecting in it "a human face, wearing a stiff white ruff around its neck, a black coat, and a collar that was turned up".

Horrified by what he'd seen, he immediately left the palace, refusing to return, and was ultimately forced into giving up the lucrative contract.

Possibly the most disturbing and frequent apparition is that of the figure of a broken woman, commonly known as Agnes.

Agnes's story starts in 1590, eleven miles to the east of Holyrood in the small village of Tranent.

Tortured and tried as a witch during the North Berwick Witch Trials, Agnes Sampson was strangled and then burned at the stake in 1591.

This was not to be the end of Agnes, however, as soon after her pitiful apparition began to appear.

Over the past 430 years, Agnes has been seen in numerous places around Edinburgh, but, most surprisingly, she has been seen in Holyrood Palace, even into the present day.

In the 1990s, a young German diplomat had a chilling encounter with Agnes's apparition, prompting a hasty retreat from the room. He recounted a harrowing sight: a bald, naked spectre ominously advancing toward him.

Agnes made her most recent appearance in 2014, when a maintenance worker, tasked with duties at the palace after hours, spotted her at the far end of a brightly illuminated corridor. She again appeared bald, naked, and grievously wounded, her limping figure slowly approaching the startled man with outstretched arms. The witness screamed in terror at what he was witnessing, and just as suddenly as she had appeared, Agnes vanished into thin air.

Why Agnes is seen in Holyrood, no one quite knows. If we look back to the origin of the North Berwick Witch Trials, it may help us understand why, and it may change our belief that it's not the location she haunted, but a person.

The witch trials were instigated by King James the 6th, a fervent believer in witches, who had been the apparent target of a wicked storm conjured by the accused witches while crossing the North Sea from Denmark back home to Scotland.

King James lived in Holyrood at the time of Agnes's torture and barbaric death.

Perhaps her spirit came back to visit on James some of the torment she had endured in death, or perhaps she came back to confront him with the horror of his actions.

The true intentions behind her haunting may forever remain a mystery.

No stately home would be complete without the ghost of a lady in grey, and Holyrood is no different to the likes of both Edinburgh and Glamis Castle.

Witnesses claim that a "Grey Lady" has been sighted wandering the palace's corridors and rooms.

She is often described as wearing a grey gown, which gives her the name. Some say she appears to be in sixteenth-century attire, while others simply see her as a shimmering, ghostly presence.

Unlike some of the more notorious spirits, the Grey Lady is not associated with any tragic or horrifying events. Instead, she's often considered a benign presence.

Witnesses report her as a peaceful, protective spirit. She's been seen looking out of windows and gliding gracefully through the hallways.

Visitors to Holyrood Palace, both guests and staff, continue to share their encounters with the Grey Lady. Some mention unexplained cold spots and the sensation of being watched, especially in the vicinity of her appearances.

While the Grey Lady's identity remains a mystery, some speculate she could be a former servant or lady-in-waiting to Mary, Queen of Scots.

It's clear that this historic site holds more than just royal tales. While Holyrood Abbey and Palace are known for their role in Scotland's history, it's the whispered stories within their walls that truly capture my attention.

In including these forgotten ghost stories in my book, I aim to shed light on the overlooked narratives that enrich our understanding of these places. Holyrood's haunted history speaks to something deeper – a connection to the past that reminds us of the power of storytelling.

CHAPTER 7
CLOSING

In Edinburgh's Old Town, where narrow closes and towering tenements define the landscape, the ghosts of the past are ever-present. This historic area was once home to a bustling community of tens of thousands of men, women, and children, whose lives were intertwined with and often dependent on the very streets they walked. But amid the crowded thoroughfares and cramped living conditions, life was harsh, unforgiving, and sometimes tragically short.

For generations, residents of the Old Town endured squalor and poverty, with sanitation virtually non-existent and disease rampant. Rats scurried through the streets, and the air was thick with the stench of human waste. In such conditions, death was a constant companion, claiming lives with alarming frequency. Crime was also a prevalent issue, with theft, violence, and other criminal activities occurring regularly in the narrow, shadowy closes. The Old Town was a place where survival often meant engaging in or falling victim to unlawful acts.

The area has undergone continuous cycles of construction and destruction over time, reflecting Edinburgh's often violent past. Edinburgh Castle, as previously mentioned, holds the distinction of being the most besieged building in Great Britain. The burning of Edinburgh in 1544 by forces under Henry VIII is another example of the city's enduring trials. These events provide insight into the tumultuous history of Edinburgh, helping us to understand its complex narrative.

The stories I've shared offer just a small glimpse of the numerous tales associated with this incredibly haunted area. While the area is widely known for its hauntings, I don't think the volume of stories is truly understood by those with a passing interest in ghost stories. When I first started collecting and telling these stories, to help me visualise the hotspots, I plotted the locations on a map of Edinburgh with pins marking every haunted site I knew. Due to the sheer volume of tales, some on the same street and even in the same building, I'm now almost out of pins. The abundance of hauntings in this area is undeniable. It's no wonder that the ghosts of Edinburgh's Old Town seem to linger, their restless spirits tethered to the places they once called home. They are the echoes of those who lived and died in this ancient city, their stories etched into the very walls that surround us.

As we wander through the shadowy alleyways and hidden closes, let us remember the thousands who came before us, whose lives were shaped by the harsh realities of life in the Old Town. Their presence serves as a reminder of the resilience of the human spirit and the enduring legacy of Edinburgh's storied past.

In our next section, we will escape the narrow confines of the

Old Town and explore the wide, leafy spaces of Edinburgh's "New Town" and beyond.

PART TWO
BEYOND THE OLD TOWN
FORGOTTEN HAUNTS OF EDINBURGH

As we venture beyond the ancient cobblestone streets and towering tenements and spires of Edinburgh's Old Town, we uncover a realm of forgotten haunts and overlooked stories that have faded into obscurity. From the grand, wide Georgian streets of the historic New Town to the rugged cliffs of Salisbury Crags, Edinburgh's lesser-known corners harbour secrets that hint at ghosts and echoes of the past.

With the "Act of Union" between Scotland and England signed in 1707 and the threat of war lessening, Edinburgh was able to expand beyond its cramped ancient confines, and the New Town was born. The construction of Edinburgh's New Town began in the late eighteenth century as a response to overcrowding and unsanitary conditions in the Old Town. Led by architect James Craig, the New Town was designed to provide a solution to these urban challenges while showcasing the city's grandeur and elegance, bringing light and space to those who could afford it. Craig's plan involved laying out a grid of streets and squares, with spacious neoclassical buildings constructed from locally quarried sandstone. Wealthy residents and professionals flocked to the New Town, attracted by its modern amenities and stylish architecture. Over several decades, the area transformed into a vibrant cultural and commercial hub, symbolising Edinburgh's transition to a modern European capital.

Over the years, the city boundaries have spread further afield, swallowing up some of the outlying villages like Leith, Stockbridge, Morningside, and Comiston, blending their unique histories and their own hauntings and ghost stories into the diverse fabric of Edinburgh's urban landscape. Among these tales, I remember being told of a property just off the park known as Leith Links, reputed to have regular visitations from the spirit of a monk clad in a brown habit, and even more unnervingly, a floating disembodied head. I've also had my own uncanny experience when my parents lived in Comiston.

In the winter of 1991, I had a weekend job selling trainers in a clothes shop in the Cameron Toll shopping centre. My parents were self-employed and often worked long hours, frequently staying late into the night on Fridays to get everything organised for the weekend. I normally got home around 7pm, and the first thing I'd do, what almost every teenager of the day would do, was sit down to watch some telly. At the time, TVs were big and wide with curved glass screens. As I picked up the remote to switch it on, I noticed a silhouetted figure standing in the doorway to my left. The figure looked male, about five feet nine, and appeared to be wearing an outfit reminiscent of a 1940s private detective. As I stared at the TV screen for what felt like an eternity, the figure turned and walked out the door. I remember the coat flaring out as he turned, but I don't recall hearing any footsteps. My dog, a

Siberian husky named Lobo, was in the room with me at the time but didn't react, which left me confused. I checked the doors and windows in the house, but everything was locked. Nothing else happened in that house that I'm aware of, so I wouldn't call it haunted, but it's an experience that has left me puzzled to this day.

I've previously mentioned that I mapped out the haunted locations I'm currently aware of in the Old Town on a street map of Edinburgh. I expanded this to cover the wider Edinburgh area and discovered that the New Town, particularly around the Stockbridge, Dean Village and Comely Bank areas, forms its own paranormal hotspot. If you look further afield, some of Edinburgh's more unusual legends and stories extend beyond the fortified Old Town walls, such as the mystery of the Arthur's Seat coffins and the centaur of the Edinburgh Botanical Gardens.

In 1836, a group of boys exploring Arthur's Seat in Edinburgh stumbled upon a hidden cache of seventeen miniature coffins. Each coffin, approximately 3.75 inches long, contained a small, dressed wooden figure. The purpose and origin of these coffins remain a mystery, sparking numerous theories. Some speculate they were linked to witchcraft or used as talismans, while others believe they represented victims of Burke and Hare, the infamous body snatchers. Despite extensive speculation, the true story behind these eerie artefacts remains unsolved.

Incredibly, in the 1960s, Robert Ogilvie Crombie reported encountering several mythical creatures in the Edinburgh Botanical Gardens. Among these, he claimed to have seen a centaur, a faun named Kurmos, and the Greek god Pan.

In the next set of stories, we delve into the hidden histories of forgotten landmarks and secluded corners, where the spirits of bygone eras linger, waiting to share their untold stories with those willing to listen.

Craigmillar Castle, once a formidable fortress, now stands vacant, a shell of its former self that bore witness to centuries of intrigue and mystery. Its ancient walls, for hundreds of years, saw the rise and fall of powerful families, hosted visiting monarchs and heard the whispers of treachery and betrayal.

Blacket Place, now a quiet and unassuming residential area, was once the setting for spine-tingling tales of horrifying apparitions and paranormal phenomena that terrorised a Victorian family during the late nineteenth century. It was a house where shadows shifted where no light penetrated, and whispers echoed in the stillness of the night, hinting at the restless spirits or spirit that inhabited this place.

In Stockbridge, beneath its picturesque streets and charming shops, lies a history of hauntings that defies its serene modern facade. The spirits of those who once walked its lanes now wander in the twilight, their stories waiting to be uncovered by those who dare to look beyond the surface.

George Heriot's School, a landmark of education and tradition, is not just a place of learning but also one of lingering phantoms. The echoes of the past resonate through its halls, where the spirits of former students and teachers seem to linger, bound to the institution that shaped their lives.

In Morningside, amid its leafy avenues and quaint cafes, whispers of the past intertwine with the present. Beneath the tranquil surface, hidden histories await discovery, where ghostly apparitions may still roam, preserving the secrets of this tranquil neighbourhood's past.

Come with us as we journey through Edinburgh's forgotten haunts. In this city, the line between the living and the dead blurs, and history's echoes linger in the mist. These stories show that every part of this ancient city, old and new, has a story, and the past is always present.

CHAPTER 8
CRAIGMILLAR CASTLE

Before the imposing stone walls of Craigmillar Castle graced the landscape, the area on which it now stands held a rich history of its own and was used for a very different purpose.

Prior to the construction of the castle, the land was gifted to the monks of Holyrood by King David the 1st in the 1100s. The monks owned and worked the land for the next two hundred years before part of it was then granted to the Preston family by King David the 2nd in 1342, with the remainder of the land granted to the Prestons by King Robert the 2nd in 1374. Over the next two hundred years, the Preston family fortified the area and strengthened the castle's defences. The tower house was constructed in the 1400s, and the French-inspired courtyard was constructed around a hundred years later.

Throughout the fifteenth and early sixteenth centuries, Craigmillar Castle served as a strategic stronghold, playing a crucial role in the defence of Edinburgh and the surrounding areas. Its sturdy defences made it a formidable obstacle for any would-be invaders.

During the turbulent period known as the "Rough Wooing" (which features heavily in many of Scotland's ghostly tales), orchestrated by Henry VIII of England, the English sought to exert their dominance through military force – an alliance between young Mary, Queen of Scots, and Edward, Prince of Wales. Craigmillar Castle became embroiled in this tumultuous time as English troops, led by the Earl of Hertford, left destruction in their wake, ultimately resulting in the castle's destruction on 8 May 1544. This traumatic event followed the devastating sack of Edinburgh. In the aftermath of this fiery chaos, Sir Simon Preston emerged as a central figure in the castle's history.

He undertook the extensive task of repairing and rebuilding the once formidable castle, overseeing the meticulous remodelling of the domestic quarters within its courtyard. Sir Simon Preston's legacy extended beyond the castle's stones; he assumed the role of Lord Provost of Edinburgh for several years, earning recognition as a steadfast supporter of Queen Mary. His loyalty was reciprocated when the Queen appointed him to her Privy Council – an honour that reflected his unwavering dedication to the monarchy during a time of profound upheaval.

The castle was designed not only as a defensive fortress but also as a residence befitting the status of its noble occupants. Throughout the years, the castle witnessed a series of events that reflected the shifting tides of Scottish history. In the sixteenth century, Craigmillar played host to the infamous "Craigmillar Bond"; a secret pact among nobles to remove Mary, Queen of Scots' husband, Lord Darnley, from the political scene. This pivotal event had far-reaching consequences, shaping the course of Scotland's monarchy. By the seventeenth century, the castle had transitioned from a military stronghold to a grand country residence, evolving to suit the changing needs and tastes of its inhabitants. As time marched on, the castle's significance began to wane, and by the eighteenth century, it had fallen into a state of disrepair.

In the following centuries, it changed hands several times, and its fortunes ebbed and flowed. The once-mighty fortress became a romantic ruin, captivating the imaginations of poets, writers, and travellers who wandered through its echoing halls. Today, Craigmillar Castle stands as a testament to the layers of history that have shaped Scotland's story. With its grand towers, enigmatic hidden chambers, and panoramic vistas, Craigmillar Castle evokes a palpable sense of awe and mystery. These very features that command our fascination also serve as the haunting grounds for spirits that linger from times long past.

When the image of a haunted castle forms in your mind, it's likely to be one of broken battlements and ruined towers shrouded in a drifting mist, where moonlight weaves enigmatic shadows through the remnants. That was the scene one night in May 1934, when a couple of locals were out enjoying a late night stroll in the farmers' fields surrounding the castle. As they neared the castle, their attention was suddenly captivated by a distant, yet distinct, movement. Their eyes strained and torches poised, they directed their beams towards the source of the movement, revealing a solitary, shadowy figure gradually approaching the ancient castle's ruins. Suspecting this was another walker, someone they may well have known, they called out to them…but received no recognition in return.

As they continued to observe the silent figure, a shiver ran down their spines – whomever they were observing wasn't walking, they were floating. Watching, wide-eyed in amazement, the floating spectre moved through the ruins of the castle and disappeared through one of the many ancient doorways. Feeling as courageous as they were curious, they decided to chase the uncanny visitor into the depths of the castle, but no matter where they looked, there was no one to be seen. The realisation soon hit the men that what they had witnessed wasn't a neighbour and it wasn't someone of flesh and blood; what they had seen was a ghostly apparition.

So frightened were they by what they had witnessed, they ran to find help, and when they did, they organised a posse of makeshift ghost hunters to investigate the castle and establish just exactly what they had witnessed. This ad hoc assembly approached the castle ruins with a blend of trepidation and scepticism, each reacting differently to the incredible tale they had been told. However, the dynamic shifted abruptly as a piercing cry shattered the stillness of the night. "GHOOOSSSSTTTT!" came the cry from one of the posse. In an instant, a surge of adrenaline propelled the men into motion, and they charged through the darkness toward the formidable ruins of the castle. One of the group had seen a dark, cloaked figure flitting in between the walls of the castle, so pointed to the area where he'd last seen it. Splitting up, they entered the ruins. Torch beams could be seen frantically moving from one area of the castle to the next. The men shined their lights into every corner and searched behind every wall, but found nothing; the figure had simply vanished.

Several months drifted by, and the events of that fateful night had begun to recede into the recesses of the witnesses' minds. Yet, as the evening of the fifth of May descended, the memories of that night would resurface with an overwhelming rush. On an evening not too dissimilar to that night a year prior, a spectral figure was again seen "floating" – only this time it wasn't among the stone walls and atmospheric ruins of the castle. This time it was on a road leading up to the castle.

On this occasion, the witnesses had a clearer and closer view of the apparition, describing it as wearing "a long dark blue hooded cloak", with "a mass of tangled black hair which falls over the forehead", while heavy riding boots with spurs adorned the spooky figure's feet. As the ethereal figure gracefully glided along the densely forested road, they stood there in sheer astonishment, captivated by the inexplicable sight before them. Slowly, the figure pivoted its head, locking its gaze upon them with malevolent eyes that seemed to "gleam menacingly at the sight of a mere mortal's approach". Prompted by the chilling confrontation, a swift response ensued as a group of brave locals initiated a fresh ghost hunt. A member of the posse did claim to see the spirit again, describing a shadowy figure that seemed to effortlessly navigate the ruins. However, despite their determined efforts, their search yielded nothing. Again, the figure managed to evade capture. This appears to be the last reported sighting of the "ghost with spurs".

Every castle, with its weathered stones and time-worn corridors, cradles the echoes of time. Within these ancient walls, tales of gallant knights and star-crossed lovers abound.

Craigmillar is no exception to this spectral tradition, and its haunting legacy is anchored by the enigmatic presence of the White Lady.

The story begins with Lady Marion, also known as Marion Shaw, a noblewoman ensnared in the throes of forbidden love. In a time when societal norms dictated every aspect of one's life, Lady Marion dared to follow her heart, falling for a man her family vehemently opposed, possibly a humble servant or a commoner. Love, however, cares little for the demands of nobility, and Lady Marion's clandestine affair was eventually uncovered. Her own father, in a heart-wrenching turn of events, felt forced to imprison his own daughter within the cold, stone walls of Craigmillar Castle.

There, in the dim confines of a small, desolate chamber, Lady Marion's world shrank to darkness, despair, and isolation. As the days turned to weeks, and weeks to months, Lady Marion's once-rosy health withered away.

Some believe she succumbed to a broken heart, while others speculate that starvation may have claimed her fragile existence. Regardless of the cause, her tragic end left an indelible mark on the castle's history.

Today, the legend of Lady Marion lives on as the White Lady, an ethereal spectre dressed in pure white. Many visitors to Craigmillar Castle have reported seeing her apparition and experiencing paranormal events within the ancient halls and grounds. Her mournful cries are said to echo through the night, reflecting her eternal sorrow. Some claim to have seen her ghostly figure near the chamber where she was once imprisoned, forever haunting the castle that was both her sanctuary and her prison.

The White Lady of Craigmillar Castle stands as a poignant reminder that love, even in its most forbidden form, can transcend time and death, leaving a lasting legacy of longing and sorrow within the castle's walls.

I've chosen to include Craigmillar Castle in this book because, while it is rightly known for its rich history and strategic importance, its ghost stories are often overlooked. I remember a school trip to Craigmillar when I was around nine. My classmates and I spent some time in the dungeon, and, as kids do, stories started to spread that a green, disembodied hand had been seen floating in a recess by the dungeon door. This was enough to send us fleeing to the safety of the teachers.

Our guide assured us there were no spooky stories associated with the castle, which reassured some of us but left me confused. Surely a place like this had to have at least one ghost story. It would be years before the onset of the internet revealed that my initial scepticism was justified. Even then, I found only a handful of sites recounting ghostly encounters.

While it's now best known as a filming location, appearing in major movies like the 2018 releases *Outlaw King* and *Mary Queen of Scots*, as well as being a prominent setting in the hit show *Outlander*, it's the castle's haunted history that has always captivated me.

By featuring Craigmillar Castle, we look beyond the veneer of tourism and TV glamour to highlight the hidden and unreported ghost stories that contribute to Scotland's haunted heritage. This offers readers a deeper understanding of the supernatural elements intertwined with the nation's historical sites.

CHAPTER 9
GEORGE HERIOT'S

The upcoming chapter features two haunted locations, diverging from the usual focus on one, yet intriguingly interconnected by their historical ties.

As discussed previously, the Rough Wooing aimed to secure Tudor dynastic stability and counterbalance France's influence in Scotland by marrying Prince Edward to the young Mary, Queen of Scots.

King Henry sought to unify Scotland with England or establish English hegemony over the kingdom. Henry declared war in December 1543, as James Hamilton, who was appointed to govern in Scotland until Mary reached adulthood, made gains against rebels supporting the English marriage. Nobles such as the Earl of Lennox, Earl of Glencairn, Earl of Cassillis, and Earl of Angus communicated with Henry VIII via messengers, requesting intervention. In March, Henry promised a significant military response.

The events of May 1544 marked a significant escalation in the conflict, as Henry's forces unleashed devastation upon Edinburgh and its surrounding areas. This would later become known as "the Burning of Edinburgh". Edward Seymour, later the Duke of Somerset, led the English army as the King's Lieutenant. The orders from Henry were to devastate the city:

> "Put all to fire and sword, burn Edinburgh, so razed and defaced when you have sacked and gotten what ye can of it, as there may remain forever a perpetual memory of the vengeance of God lightened upon [them] for their falsehood and disloyalty."

Under pressure, the Provost of Edinburgh allowed the English to plunder both Leith and Edinburgh, resulting in the city being set ablaze on 7 May. Seymour proposed capturing Cardinal Beaton, the Archbishop of St Andrews, a supporter of the Auld Alliance with France, during the invasion.

Despite the English assault, the Scottish artillery within Edinburgh Castle continued to harass the English forces, preventing them from besieging the castle due to their limited time and resources. The English fleet departed with plundered goods, including two ships belonging to James V of Scotland.

This event was the first act in a turbulent period in Anglo-Scottish relations, with both sides enduring years of warfare and political manoeuvring in pursuit of their respective goals.

Following Henry's command to burn Edinburgh, English troops expanded their devastation to the nearby areas, employing scorched-earth tactics. About five miles northwest of the city, Cramond, safeguarded by Lauriston Castle, suffered the brunt of their assault, leading to the destruction of the town and the castle itself.

Although records are sparse, we know Lauriston Castle was originally constructed sometime in the late mediaeval period. Following its sacking in 1544, it remained in ruins for nearly fifty years until Sir Archibald Napier initiated construction of a Tower House in 1590. This marked the beginning of a new chapter in the castle's history, as it underwent significant renovations and expansions over the centuries. The Napiers, a prominent Scottish family, held ownership of the castle for generations, contributing to its architectural evolution and shaping its role in local history. Throughout its existence, Lauriston Castle has witnessed numerous events and transitions, reflecting the broader changes in Scottish society and politics.

Lauriston Castle is also believed to be haunted.

One of the most well-known ghost stories linked to Lauriston Castle revolves around the figure of a woman known as Janet, often referred to as "the Grey Lady". According to local lore, Janet was a servant at the castle who fell deeply in love with the master of the house. When her affections were not returned, Janet was overwhelmed with despair and tragically ended her own life by jumping from the tower. Since then, her spirit is said to linger within the castle, manifesting as fleeting glimpses of a sorrowful figure drifting through the corridors, her presence accompanied by a chilling sensation that lingers long after she disappears from view. Despite the passage of centuries, Janet's restless spirit continues to haunt Lauriston Castle, a poignant reminder of love unrequited and the enduring power of the human heart's deepest emotions. She's also believed to have been caught on camera.

In January 2020 Drew McAdam captured a curious image while waiting at Lauriston Castle in Edinburgh for an event. Arriving early, he took several photos of the landmark before the custodian arrived to deactivate the alarm and unlock the building. Upon reviewing the pictures later, McAdam was astonished by what he discovered.

In one of his images, a figure dressed in what appeared to be outdated clothing was clearly visible standing at a window. Sharing the photo and recounting the experience on social media, McAdam asserted, "I have not edited this photo in any way. It is exactly as it came on the camera." He further explained that there was no one else present in the building at the time. If an unauthorised individual had somehow gained access, the motion-sensor alarm protecting the castle would have been triggered.

In August 2023, another apparition was apparently captured on camera by a couple on one of the many guided tours of the castle and its grounds.

Stewart Ross and his fiancée, Bianka Horel, were in the castle's kitchen area when they took a picture of what they believe to be the apparition of what they describe as a mother and child.

Stewart said, "I didn't feel anything at the time the photo was taken. But looking at the photo it looks like a young woman leaning or a woman holding a baby. It was actually my dad that noticed the 'ghost' in this picture that Bianka took on my phone. I sort of dismissed it right away. I have never really believed in ghosts before. I was a security guard for a few years, wandering around places at night, but not once have I felt or seen anything. But looking at the photo closely, it was actually like a magic eye photo; you can't see at first; then suddenly it's there. There was no smoke or shadow noticeable at the time, but there is in the photo."

Could the castle's bloody history have left a lasting mark, or could the Napier family's legacy extend beyond the physical realm in the form of ghosts at Lauriston Castle?

As we explore the intriguing stories surrounding Lauriston Castle and its ghostly residents, it's interesting to think about the family connections that reach far beyond its ancient walls. This brings us to George Heriot, the founder of George Heriot's School in Edinburgh. Heriot's ties to the Napiers go beyond mere historical significance; they serve as a tangible link bridging the past and present. Through his marriage to Alison Primrose, Heriot becomes intricately connected to the Napier family. Alison, descending from James Primrose of Carrington and niece to Archibald Napier of Merchiston, intertwines her family's narrative with that of the renowned mathematician John Napier, Archibald's son. Thus, the tales echoing within Lauriston Castle resonate not only with ancient legends but also with the enduring familial bonds that unite the legacies of two influential families.

As we consider the intertwined histories of Lauriston Castle and the Heriot family, it sets the stage for the next chapter in our exploration – a ghostly tale whispered through the corridors of George Heriot's School itself. Stay tuned as we uncover the mysteries that envelop these hallowed halls, revealing secrets that transcend time and space.

Situated in the heart of Edinburgh, George Heriot's School stands as a testament to centuries of academic excellence and tradition. Its storied past, dating back to the seventeenth century, intertwines with the rich mosaic of Scottish history, leaving an indelible mark on both the cityscape and the realm of education.

Founded in 1628 by George Heriot, a prominent goldsmith and jeweller to King James VI and I, the school was established with the noble purpose of providing education to Edinburgh's orphaned and fatherless children. Heriot's vision, inspired by his commitment to philanthropy and his desire to leave a lasting legacy, laid the foundation for what would become one of Scotland's most prestigious educational institutions.

Initially housed in a building near Greyfriars Kirkyard, George Heriot's School soon outgrew its humble beginnings as its reputation for academic excellence spread far and wide. In 1650, the school moved to its current location on Lauriston Place, where it occupies an impressive building inspired by the architecture of the French Renaissance.

Over the centuries, George Heriot's School has evolved and expanded, adapting to the changing needs of its students and the demands of modern education. Today, it remains committed to its founding principles of providing a high-quality education to young people from all walks of life, regardless of their background or circumstances. Its distinguished alumni include notable figures such as Sir Walter Scott, the renowned Scottish novelist and poet; Alexander Graham Bell, inventor of the telephone; James Clerk Maxwell, a pioneering physicist known for his contributions to electromagnetic theory; Ronnie Corbett, the beloved comedian and actor; and Shirley Manson, lead singer of the rock band Garbage. These individuals reflect the school's rich heritage and its enduring influence on Edinburgh's cultural and intellectual landscape.

One of the most intriguing aspects of George Heriot's School is its connection to the world of literature and popular culture. Many people believe that J. K. Rowling, the author of the Harry Potter series, drew inspiration from the school's imposing facade and majestic towers when imagining

Hogwarts School of Witchcraft and Wizardry. Although Rowling herself has never confirmed this speculation, the parallels between the two institutions are undeniable, from the grandeur of their architecture to the sense of history and tradition that permeates their halls.

Whether or not George Heriot's School served as the real-life inspiration for Hogwarts, its links to the world of Harry Potter have captured the imagination of countless fans around the globe. Today, visitors to Edinburgh can explore the school's historic grounds and imagine themselves stepping into the magical world of wizards and witches, where anything is possible.

As George Heriot's School continues to uphold its legacy of academic excellence and innovation, its ties to Harry Potter serve as a reminder of the enduring power of imagination and the transformative impact of education. From its humble beginnings to its current status as a cherished institution, George Heriot's School remains a beacon of learning and inspiration for generations to come.

Along with rumours that Heriot's acted as the inspiration for the real-life Hogwarts, there are stories that the building may have more than that in common with the famous wizard; there are stories that its hallways are teaming with ghosts.

This notion is not merely hearsay; it is supported by firsthand accounts, such as the one shared by Beverly, who spent time working within the hallowed halls of Heriot's in the 1980s.

Beverly recounts:

> "In the mid-'80s, I had just finished my two years at drama school, studying stage management, and got a job with a

youth musical theatre company, who were performing at the Edinburgh Fringe.

"It is rarely a well-paid job, doing the Edinburgh Festival, and the company offered travel, accommodation, and food for the duration of the rehearsal and performance time. As I had moved back to my parents' home in Kent and had a job starting in late September, this was an excellent way to go to the festival, not be out of pocket, and be fed!

"As the company only employed a few professional members (one being me!), it was part of the agreement that we were part of the chaperone system, as all the cast were of school age.

"We moved into the George Heriot's School for the duration of the production. I understand that the school is a boarding school, but we were all living in the classrooms.

"I was in charge of eight mid-teen girls, in a large classroom, facing the large quadrant on the ground floor, in the shadow of the castle.

"The story of the Phantom Bagpiper was told to one of the group, and the story went round like wildfire. One night after the show, everyone had gone to bed, and suddenly we could all hear the strains of a piper. But that turned out to be a false alarm – it seems the Edinburgh Tattoo rehearsals were going on, in the wee small hours, and it was the Lone Piper rehearsing at the castle!

"The room we were staying in was large with high windows. There were no curtains, so there was light almost all the time.

"There were pockets of cold in the room, which we tried to put down to the old building and the fact it was Scotland in the summer! Things would move around the room, go missing, to turn up in other parts of the room. I spent seven weeks with these young women. They were already friends anyway, and all attended the same boarding school, so they had lived together since the age of eleven, so at no time did they feel that they were either being stolen from, or been played a trick on.

"The things that went walkabout were never anything of value. Initially, I put it down to the fact the girls knew each other, and someone had borrowed each other's hairbrush or toiletry bag. Bedside books would go from the side of our beds and then be at the far end of the room. I was the deputy stage manager, which meant I 'called' the show. During a show, the person 'on the book' will be 'calling' the show. Every time scenery moves, lights change, sound cues, music starts, etc., is all one person saying go. The DSM is in every rehearsal, and everything is recorded in their script. It is the show's bible; everything regarding the running of the show is in 'the Book'. I kept it with me at all times, and people who work in live theatre know how important 'the Book' is, and wouldn't do anything to it. So when, overnight, 'the Book' went from my bedside table to onto the teacher's desk, and there were also two hairbrushes with it, I think we knew something was odd!

"Then we noticed that as we walked past the bookshelf, books would fall on the floor behind us. Obviously, we could have dislodged something as we passed, but we all felt we hadn't touched anything.

"But one morning, all nine of us witnessed the same incident. We had all been awake for a while, and were all still lying in our camp beds, talking. It was about 6am, the sun was fully up, and the room was full of the morning sunshine.

"One of the girls had had a birthday a day or so before and had been sent a bouquet of flowers through Interflora. Suddenly, on the table the flowers were standing on, the vase rose about six inches off the surface and banged loudly down on the table – as if to get our attention. The atmosphere suddenly became very heavy. The vase then shot off the table horizontally, as if snatched at a high speed. The vase then stopped in mid-air for what felt like two or three seconds and then smashed on the floor. It was as if it had been thrown to the ground by an American football player, if you understand what I mean?

"The vase smashed everywhere, with water, flowers and glass going all over our beds. Everyone leapt out of bed and rushed into the school corridor in our PJs, and it was really unnerving. Being the 'adult' in the situation, after a few minutes, I went back into the classroom, and the atmosphere had completely changed! All the negativity had lifted, and despite the broken vase all over the floor, the room felt calm and undisturbed.

"It wasn't easy going back to sleep in the room after that, and no one wanted to be there on their own, so we were divided up and put into other rooms, and we finished our run in Edinburgh about three days later.

"All of us had thought we had seen a dark tall shadow, from the corner of our eye, and it wasn't easy to try to convince teenage girls that it was nothing to be concerned about.

"I only saw 'the shape' personally twice. It was very quick, tall, and shapeless. It felt male, although I saw no features. A couple of the girls expressed they felt a man was watching them, but it didn't feel sexual – and at the start, didn't feel menacing – that built up and was at its peak with the flowers. Then completely gone!"

Beverly's account offers a glimpse into the haunting events that many believe have been reported within the walls of George Heriot's School over the years. While some may dismiss such stories as mere folklore or the product of overactive imaginations, others believe that they provide evidence of a supernatural presence lingering within the ancient building.

Could these strange happenings be attributed to the restless spirits of former inhabitants, or is there a more rational explanation waiting to be uncovered? Whatever the truth may be, one thing is certain: the mysteries of George Heriot's School continue to captivate and intrigue all who dare to explore its shadowy corridors and hidden passageways.

Given Heriot's location, right next to Greyfriars, sharing a boundary wall, it's hardly surprising it has its own dark and terrifying supernatural stories. The close connection between these sites suggests that ghosts may not respect physical boundaries like walls, implying that the land itself could hold lingering hauntings that transcend architectural divisions.

I was thrilled when Beverly contacted me with her experiences. These are exactly the kind of unreported phenomena that I love to hear about and shine a light on.

With so much history around Edinburgh, I'm convinced that people experience some kind of haunting event almost daily, perhaps without even noticing until afterwards. I hope more people come forward with their own tales of spooky encounters.

CHAPTER 10
BLACKET PLACE

Edinburgh is renowned for many things; its people and the city itself have played a pivotal role in shaping the world for centuries, continuing to influence the modern world. In the 1700s, Edinburgh emerged as a hub for intellectual and philosophical advancements, making significant contributions to the broader Enlightenment movement.

Enlightenment thinkers promoted concepts such as human rights, secularism, and political philosophy, influencing the development of constitutional governance and the critique of absolutism.

The University of Edinburgh's medical school produced notable figures like Alexander Fleming, the discoverer of penicillin, and Joseph Lister, a pioneer in antiseptic surgery.

The city stands as a muse to countless wordsmiths who have left their mark on the world of literature. From the intellectual gatherings of the Enlightenment to the mysterious closes of the Old Town, this city has inspired and housed some of the greatest literary minds. Influential writers such as Sir Walter

Scott, Muriel Spark, and Irvine Welsh have all called Edinburgh home. Another literary giant whom Edinburgh can claim as its own is Sir Athur Conan Doyle.

Sir Arthur Conan Doyle remains one of the city's most celebrated contributors to the global literary landscape. Born in 1859, in Picardy Place, Doyle had a troubled early life due to his father's struggles with alcohol. Due to this in 1864, the family separated, and the children found temporary accommodations throughout Edinburgh. Arthur, at one point, lived with Mary Burton, the aunt of a friend, at Liberton Bank House on Gilmerton Road, in the south of the city, all the while pursuing his studies at Newington Academy, living there until 1867 when the family were reunited.

Financed by wealthy uncles, Doyle was sent down to England at the age of nine to attend the Jesuit preparatory school Hodder Place, Stonyhurst in Lancashire, studying there until 1875. From 1875 to 1876, he furthered his education at a Jesuit school in Austria; then from 1876 to 1881, Doyle studied medicine at the University of Edinburgh Medical School.

Despite his Catholic upbringing, Doyle eventually renounced the faith and embraced agnosticism, with some people attributing this shift to his time spent studying in the less rigid Austrian school. In later years, he delved into spiritualist mysticism.

These days he is best known for creating the iconic detective Sherlock Holmes, a character who has transcended literature to become a cultural phenomenon. The detective's keen powers of observation and deductive reasoning have left an indelible mark on the mystery genre.

The genesis for Holmes is often attributed to Dr Joseph Bell, a prominent figure from Edinburgh who is said to have inspired the character.

Dr Bell was a lecturer at the University of Edinburgh Medical School when Conan Doyle studied there. He was known for his keen powers of observation, logical reasoning, and deductive methods, which greatly influenced the creation of Holmes and are attributes Holmes is often celebrated for.

Doyle once remarked that Bell "often learned little tricks from his old master" and credited Bell with shaping Holmes's analytical and deductive techniques.

Bell, throughout his career, participated in numerous police inquiries, primarily within Scotland, including the 1893 Ardlamont mystery, often collaborating with forensic specialist Professor Henry Littlejohn.

The Ardlamont mystery of 1893 involved a controversial shooting incident at Ardlamont House in Scotland. The case centred around allegations of foul play in the death of Lieutenant Alfred Monson's friend, Cecil Hambrough, during a hunting expedition. The trial garnered significant attention due to suspicions of a staged crime scene and questions about Monson's involvement. Ultimately, the outcome of the trial was acquittal for Monson, but the case remains shrouded in mystery and controversy.

Additionally, Bell provided his insights on the 1888 Ripper murders to Scotland Yard.

Beyond medicine, Bell made significant contributions to the field of forensics and maintained a successful medical career, leaving a lasting legacy in both the medical and literary worlds.

Dr Bell famously lived in a large townhouse in Melville Crescent, but prior to this he owned a large corner property in the Newington area of the city, on a street called Blacket Place.

Until the sixteenth century, Newington was part of the ancient forest of Drumselch, with only Grange of St Giles and the roads via Liberton and Dalkeith interrupting the woodland.

During the seventeenth and eighteenth centuries, gallows stood in the area known as Gibbet Load.

In 1805, Benjamin Bell, great-grandfather to Dr Joseph Bell, purchased the entire Newington estate, constructing Newington House, marking a period of intense development in the eighteenth and early nineteenth centuries.

While an affluent area, it could not escape scandal, and in 1829, after the execution of the infamous body snatcher William Hare, a mob surrounded Robert Knox's house on Newington Road, burning an effigy of the good doctor. Knox, as cunning as he was clever, was able to escape by disguising himself as a Highlander and fleeing the area.

Blacket Place, built between 1830 and 1850 and sheltered from the main road by large protective walls, was the centre of a spine-chilling haunting in the late 1880s, documented by the Society for Psychical Research.

Turning into Blacket Place, you pass through the old entry gate that once safeguarded the street from the busy Dalkeith Road. Here you'll find many large Georgian and Victorian townhouses lining this quiet and well-to-do street. One house, set a little back from the entrance, had been happily occupied by an unnamed family since 1871.

On the face of it, the three-story sandstone house was as impressive and normal as the other houses on the street, and for many years life in the house was as you would expect – normal.

However, as the clock ticked towards the late 1880s, peculiar occurrences began to cast a shadow over the once-tranquil facade of this mysterious house.

Local whispers spoke of strange sights in the dead of night, unsettling events unfolding behind tightly drawn curtains, and an unsettling chill that lingered even on the warmest days.

The rumours caught the attention of a Mrs Brietzcke of the Society for Psychical Research (SPR), prompting an investigation into the unexplained phenomena that seemed to converge within the walls of this unsuspecting residence.

What they uncovered would not only challenge the boundaries of the known, but etch Blacket Place into the annals of history as a place where the mundane and the supernatural collided in a haunting tale that defied explanation.

The following accounts are taken from the letters submitted to the SPR by the family themselves and can be found in the SPR archives.

Although they are not named in the journal, with the help of John Tantallon from North Edinburgh Nightmares, we have been able to uncover two of three names.

The first account is from a Miss PM. For our purposes, we will call her Miss Penelope Munro:

> "MY DEAR MRS BRIETZCKE (Brietzcke), – As I have promised, I must write you an account of the things we saw

in our old house in Edinburgh; but remember, I put them down to indigestion, or else neuralgia.

"The house was very damp, and had been unlet for a long time before we took it, which was in 1871.

"I believe I was the first who saw anything unusual, and it must have been in one autumn afternoon, about 4 p.m.

"I was passing through the hall from the dining-room to the schoolroom, where two doors faced each other, and I saw the figure of a woman, above the medium size, standing on about the fourth step from the bottom; she had her arms folded, and was draped all over (head included) in white; she seemed to be watching me, and the thrill that ran through me made me fly into the schoolroom; but almost immediately after, I ran out again to see if it was only fancy; and found it had disappeared.

"I never mentioned this to the others, or the servants, as I was so ashamed of myself, but told my mother only; but as it eventually proved, it appeared to nearly all in the house.

"I can only recollect seeing it about six or seven times altogether, I think, and it was nearly always in daylight.

"One evening when the upper hall was dark, I saw it, and had the courage to follow it, and ran straight against a shut door, which shock brought me to myself, and it disappeared.

"Another afternoon I saw it in the drawing-room, and it was crouching over the fire; but I am sorry to say I was too great a coward to go up to it, as I could understand things appearing at night, but when they came in daylight I could not make head or tail of it.

"Another peculiar incident took place.

"Our store-room was upstairs, as the basement was so damp, and my sister had gone upstairs to get some wine.

"We heard a tremendous fall, and running out, found my sister lying at the bottom of the staircase surrounded with broken bottles and debris.

"The first thing that attracted my attention was this same figure standing just at the bend of the staircase, and, naturally enough, thought she had seen it there too, and in her fright had fallen; but when she came to, she said that somebody had pushed her at the bend and she had fallen headlong.

"I did not mention what I had seen then, as some visitors were with us, but afterwards told her; and she said she had not seen anything, but had had a blow in her back, and had fallen so marvellously that she had not hurt herself.

"Some time before this happened she had felt a hand laid upon her head in the schoolroom, and turned sick, and had seen a white figure going out of the door. Each one of us saw this figure without telling the other, and each new servant also.

"Our names were often called, and the voice nearly always came from the dining-room. Of ten and of ten we had answered and gone into the room to find it empty, servants likewise.

"On going up and down stairs, with our hands on the bannisters, we sometimes imagined a cold soft hand was laid on them, so that I avoided touching the bannisters at all.

"We had our heads often touched, and in my case, I used to feel all five fingers distinctly.

"One afternoon, while studying at the school-room table, I had stopped up my ears with my fingers. I felt my head seized very roughly, and noticing my sister had gone to the cupboard behind me, thought it was her who had touched me, so I moved my head about to escape her, and said, 'Don't,' and was recalled to myself by the governess, who touched me, and asked what on earth was the matter with me; and I found out that my sister had been back to her place for some time; that was the most distinct time that I felt it.

"I saw many other things, but they had no sequence, and so will not be interesting. Our cat was sometimes in a great fright, her hair all standing on end, and grovelling; but at those times we saw nothing, but of course felt 'skeery'.

"The bathroom first attracted my attention. We had all a great repugnance to enter it, and I was so certain that there was something uncanny about it that I asked mamma if there was a story attached to it.

"She said, 'No.' Not content with that, I investigated the room, and found out the door had been forced; and it proved that the lady who had had the house before us had drowned herself in the bath.

"Now this is a thing I cannot account for. One night, mamma as usual went at the usual hour to have her bath; and finding to her surprise the door locked, rattled it, and said, 'Come, Emmie, I want to come in.' Emily replied from the next bedroom that she was not there.

"She tried the door and then went to see where my other sister and I were. We all came out and had a try at it. I must say I could have sworn the door was locked, it might have got stuck in some peculiar way, but anyhow, after we had all left it alone if half opened itself.

"My mother certainly was puzzled at that, and she was a very practical woman. She never would acknowledge that she saw anything, but heard all the noises that we heard, and said she would move out of the house earlier than she intended, because the servants declared the house was haunted, and said they would not stay; and she was afraid of its having a bad effect upon us.

"Nothing would induce the servants to stir out of the kitchen or their bedroom after 10.30 at night; they barricaded up their door.

"One night the cook, a new servant there, was taking up some hot water bottles to our rooms, and on drawing herself up when she came to the top landing, found herself in front of this white figure; she turned tail and flew for her life to the kitchen. Hearing the noise, I ran down to see what was the matter, and we found her white and scared in the kitchen.

"We had not told her anything about the house; it is possible the other servant may have done so, although she declared she had not.

"We heard the rustling of leaves, or of a silk train on the staircase at nights, and that was the only noise that was heard in the lower regions.

"The dining-room flat was the noisiest; we heard doors opening and shutting, or at least what sounded like it, for I used to go down sometimes to try and discover what it was.

"The noises were too substantial to be cats or rats, it was more like the big heavy table in the dining-room, and the chairs being bumped about.

"At about six in the morning a heavy bump sounded, which shook the whole house; in the different rooms it sounded in different directions; and we never could find out what occasioned it, although we tried to investigate it over and over again. The shock may have taken place in some other house, and our foundations being very old, and I daresay shaky, it travelled along, and so we heard it; it was like a miniature explosion.

"We had a great aversion to the drawing-room, too, and never would sit there alone; for we had a peculiar feeling that somebody was in the room with us; I often thought I was touched, and felt somebody moving about the room.

"It was in that room that I saw a tall blue shape with what looked like eyes; but I kept looking at it, and it slowly disappeared; this was in daylight also.

"Those sort of ghostly things did not terrify me much, and especially at the last, for I was so certain that some trick was being played upon us; and tried to find out how they appeared. But one evening I was terrified by something out of the ordinary.

"I was all alone in the dining-room one night, as the others were all out at a concert, and the little one had gone to bed. It must have been about 9.30 or 10. I was working, and was opposite the press, or cupboard, the door of which was open.

"Gradually the feeling came over me that I was not alone in the room, and that I was being watched, so that I could not help raising my head, and exactly opposite me, just appearing round the press-door, was the face of a man – the most wicked and evil-looking face I have ever seen, more like a demon's face than anything else.

"The skin was of a yellowy colour, and it had black hair, moustache and beard. The eyes were fixed upon me, and even as I looked, this awful head projected more round the door, and I saw the neck.

"There we gazed at each other. I was perfectly frozen with horror, and could not move or speak.

"As soon as my senses began to collect themselves, I thought, that can't be a ghost, for it isn't transparent like the others; it seemed a solid head, for it hid the part of the door it was in front of; so I thought the best thing was to appear not frightened, as I had read in story books; so after gazing at me for what appeared a quarter-of-an-hour in my great horror, the head suddenly drew back.

"I still sat petrified, expecting it to come out again; and there I sat until the others came home, and only then went up to the door, and was not a bit surprised to find nothing behind, because the press was filled with shelves, and it was an impossibility for anybody to get into it; so it must have been a bit of my brain in an excitable condition. That was a substantial ghost, as I call it.

"I saw one other, but it was a most natural one. Passing through the hall, I saw an old woman standing by the hall door; and going to mamma I asked her who she was, and what she had come for.

"Mamma said she did not know anybody had come; so going out into the hall I saw her (the woman) still there, and went down to tell the servants that somebody had come, and to go and see what she wanted. When I came back, the woman had disappeared. I immediately went to the hall-door, found it locked, and opening it went into the garden, looking for the woman; but she was not to be seen.

"The servants, too, did not know anything about her. I had

not any fear or surprise at seeing her, because I did not guess for a moment that she was not real.

"Now I have told you all as well as I can remember it; but we put a great deal of it down to a damp house and neuralgia, and indigestion. I was constantly suffering from neuralgia there, and that, I daresay, was the cause of all my apparitions. I hope, though, that these ridiculous notes maybe of some use to you."

Penelope's sister Emily detailed her accounts:

"I have been a long time in writing out my account. I hope now it is done it will prove to be something 'not too utterly ridiculous'. It seems so foolish for a sensible creature like myself to commit to paper things so perfectly puerile.

"My contempt for ghosts passes description, and I am very angry that I did see that mournful white thing by the dressing-table, as I have to put it down; but I attribute it, like Mr Scrooge, to 'a piece of undigested beef, or speck of mustard', from which delicacies Old Marley was supposed to have been compounded. In accordance with Mrs Brietzcke's request, I send an account of my experiences at our old house in Edinburgh.

"I was quite a child when we first went there, and was told nothing as to the rumours afloat about the house, or the earlier experiences of my sisters.

"I 'felt' long before I 'saw', but thought it was merely the natural childish fear of dark rooms, and solitude, but as I grew older and stronger, I lost the fear, but not the 'feeling', which was distinctly attached to certain portions of the house, namely, the drawing-room, the dining-room, and the staircase.

"In the drawing-room the sensation was of someone pacing the room hurriedly up and down, pausing now and again, then continuing. On one occasion my eldest sister left the piano at which she was practising, because she had the distinct impression of someone passing continually behind her chair. In the dining-room I have frequently experienced the sensation of someone bending over my shoulder, a distinct feeling of the air being disturbed.

"The cat has often risen from the rug, on which it was sleeping; with hair and tail erect, in evident horror at something; and we had several cats in rotation, and each in turn exhibited symptoms of fear occasionally.

"The staircase seemed to be the happy hunting ground of the ghosts, and here repeated phenomena took place.

"Descending one evening, a small cold hand was laid upon mine, which was resting on the bannister.

"Each finger I felt exactly, soft and cold, and could hardly believe that nothing was visible.

"Others in the house frequently saw the white figure on the staircase, but I never did, and refused to believe in it at all, until one afternoon when I was sent into my mother's room to report if the fire were burning satisfactorily.

"Being disturbed in the middle of my singing, I went to execute the errand in a frame of mind, not exactly calculated to 'see ghosts'. It was dusk as I entered the room, and everything was more or less in shadow, which perhaps served to throw out in bold relief the tall white form of a woman, leaning against the window curtain by the dressing-table.

"It was supernaturally tall, and stood with arms folded, looking straight at me, with a most heartbroken expression in the eyes. Even at the first glance it did not look real, as the dark blue curtain was visible all through it, but less so at the face and shoulders. The face was so sad and sweet I did not feel very frightened, but walked straight up to the curtain, and grasped it in my hands, shook it, and looked behind it, but there was nothing there. I was frightened then, and ran out of the room. I never saw it before, and never saw it after that.

"My room was at the end of a passage which led from the staircase landing and passed the bath-room door; it was only separated therefore from the bathroom by the wall, and although I knew later on what tragedy had occurred in that room, its close proximity did not disturb me in the slightest.

"My room was distinctly one of the clear spots in the house. I was always glad to get into it and close the door, as it always felt 'safe'. This feeling did not prevent me from hearing what occurred in the rest of the house.

"One night I started up in bed from a sound sleep. I do not know what woke me, but I heard a soft rustling sound descending the stairs. I could not account for it, and could only compare it to dead leaves being swept down the steps.

"Soon after, the hall clock struck 1 o'clock. The next morning, the cook and housemaid told me (of their own accord) that as the clock struck 1, they heard 'a soft rustly kind of sound come down the kitchen stairs, sweep into the laundry, run round three times, then there was a great bang!'

"The cook described the sound as 'a lot of dead leaves like!' This is very remarkable, as my room was two storeys above the kitchen, and the time and description of sound tally exactly.

"I was present when the door of the bathroom refused to open, and was about to try to open it myself for the third time, when it opened gently and resistlessly without any effort on my part. I was the only one in the house however who never heard the 'morning bang' as we called it, though the German governess and various visitors all heard it.

"We left the house earlier than we intended, as the servants refused at last to remain, and became very troublesome, never venturing about the house except in couples, and no power upon earth could have induced them to quit their room after half past 10, which from their account was in a sort of besieged garrison condition, the door being securely barricaded from within, so any disturbance which occurred during the night could not possibly be placed, as some have supposed, to their account.

"I do not think I have anything more to say. We were all glad to leave the house, and a month or two after, we went over to it one day with some friends, and the feeling of gloom and oppression was appalling, and were glad to get back into the sunshine, and all unhesitatingly pronounced it 'haunted'. It must have been fearfully damp; a bonbon left on the shelf of the cupboard in my sisters' room would be completely melted in two days, and boots and shoes, unless constantly worn, were apt to get all mouldy and damp.

"I cannot account for anything which happened, and can safely affirm that anything which I saw or felt was certainly not due to fear or nervousness, as I unhesitatingly would go to any portion of the house all alone, in the dark.

"My 'double' or 'wraith' was twice seen upon the bend of the staircase, once by my sister, and once by a friend, at different times, but upon always the same place.

> "The cook who was with us at the time of which I speak is dead, and we have lost sight of the housemaid. As I have nothing more to say, I will end."

Another sister – Zoi – added:

> "I was 10 years old at the time I saw this figure, and my mind was far from ghosts, as my mother had never allowed anyone to speak to me of such things. One day I was let out of the school-room for half-an-hour's play at 12 o'clock.
>
> "My playroom was upstairs, and as children often do, I ran upstairs on all fours, that is on my hands as well as my feet. As I reached the middle of the stairs a peculiar feeling made me look up to the top landing, and standing close to the first step of the stairs was a tall white figure of a woman, and it seemed to be above the usual height. I could see the form distinctly, but at the same time I saw through her.
>
> "It looked at me for a few seconds, then turned and walked into the passage leading to the bathroom. Not knowing what it was, I had not the slightest fear, and I followed it there. Of course, when I got there, the room was empty. It was then for the first time that I felt, as the Scotch say, 'uncanny'. I told my mother what I had seen, but she laughed at me, and soon I forgot all about it.
>
> "This is the only time I saw the figure, but I often heard myself called from a sunk press in the dining-room, but that may have been an echo.
>
> "Very frequently in the morning, about 6, my mother and I heard a loud thud against the inner wall of the house (it was a house standing in its own grounds); it shook the whole house, and for a long time my mother took no notice of it; she thought it was the servant cleaning the schoolroom

> below, and after pulling out the grand piano to clean behind, had rolled it back with too great a force, and knocked the wall.
>
> "My sisters heard it, too, but in different parts of the house. One morning my sister went down to find out if it was the servant; but she found her at the grate cleaning the irons. She said she had been there fully 10 minutes and had never heard the sound herself.
>
> "A great many of our servants left us because of these sounds and sights.
>
> "One cook we had was taking the hot water bottles up to the beds one night and she saw this figure on the middle of the stairs, and she was so frightened that she did not know she had let one of the bottles fall on her bare arm till she got downstairs again and found her arm most frightfully burnt.
>
> "Except for hearing strange sounds, which I was told to put down to rats, and having a peculiar depressed feeling come over me when I entered the house, nothing else happened to me that I can remember."

In their townhouse on Blacket Place, the Munro sisters found themselves entwined in a complex blend of the mundane and the mysterious. Penelope's tale of encountering an apparition in the schoolroom, followed by a similar incident on the staircase, paints a clear picture of supernatural encounters that defy rational explanation.

The Blacket Place haunting embodies the quintessential Victorian ghost story, yet it remains largely forgotten. It wasn't until I immersed myself in Eerie Edinburgh, shifting from a casual reader to an avid enthusiast exploring everything about haunted Edinburgh, that I stumbled upon this tale, and it immediately became a favourite. I was captivated not only by the chilling encounters of the family but also by the near obscurity of this haunting. I have passed this location hundreds of times over the years but knew nothing of its haunted past.

What fascinates me most is how it encapsulates Victorian-era beliefs and fears surrounding the supernatural, rendering it both historically and culturally significant. This eerie account involves apparitions and unexplained occurrences that deeply unsettled a family in the late nineteenth century, echoing the era's profound intrigue with ghostly tales and the mysteries beyond.

Including it in this book allows me to share a piece of forgotten history and shed light on a haunting that deserves to be remembered from an area of Edinburgh not known for its supernatural tales. This haunting exemplifies the kind of rich, yet overlooked, ghost stories that add depth to Edinburgh's haunted heritage.

CHAPTER 11
ROYAL CIRCUS

STOCKBRIDGE IS LOCATED a mile or two north of Edinburgh city centre, along the banks of the Water of Leith. This neighbourhood has a rich history that goes beyond its current role as a vibrant urban area. Originally, Stockbridge existed as a separate village, distinct from the bustling city of Edinburgh. Eventually, in 1831, Stockbridge was officially amalgamated into Edinburgh, becoming an integral part of the expanding city.

This integration marked a significant juncture in Stockbridge's history, as it transitioned from a standalone village to an essential component of Edinburgh's diverse urban landscape. The name "Stockbridge" derives from the Scots words "stock", meaning a timber footbridge, and "bryg", meaning bridge. The village's growth was closely tied to its location along the Water of Leith, facilitating trade and contributing to its development as a prosperous community. Due to its position, it was key in supporting the local mills dotted along the waterway. Stockbridge evolved into an attractive residential area, characterised by elegant Georgian and Victorian architecture. For those who are fans of rugby, Raeburn Place is the site where the first Calcutta cup match was played in 1879. Today, it stands as a testament to the enduring spirit of Edinburgh's neighbourhoods, blending history with contemporary vitality, but like many such areas, it also has a darker side.

One notable, terrible chapter in Stockbridge's history delves into the disturbing events surrounding a house on Cheyne Street. In October 1888, a group of young friends decided to fashion a makeshift football from an oilskin bundle they stumbled upon in the lane behind Cheyne Street. After kicking the "ball" around for a while, the bundle fell apart and exposed something that would horrify them and leave a stain on the area for years to come. Inside, they made a horrifying discovery – the lifeless body of a deceased child. This shocking find prompted an immediate alert to the authorities, and suspicion swiftly turned toward Jessie King and her partner, Thomas Pearson, who owned the lodging house close to where the bundle of rags was found. The truth that unfolded was hard to comprehend: the lodging house at 4 Cheyne Street, where the owners seemingly offered accommodation for unwed mothers and their infants, engaged in a far more sinister practice.

Under the guise of providing care for the infants, the owners engaged in a macabre operation known as baby farming. King and Pearson scoured the local newspapers for adverts posted by desperate mothers who, for whatever reason, were unable to care for their children and so put them up for adoption. Responding to the adverts, they promised to take the child and raise them as their own. Something the desperate mothers were keen to do; after all, this couple on the face of things looked like a well-to-do Victorian couple and gave off the air of respectability. Tragically, the reality was far more nefarious. The conditions within the lodging house were deplorable, and many infants faced neglect, malnutrition, and even death. The squalid conditions came to light when the lifeless bodies of several infants were discovered in Jessie King's residence.

The shocking revelation sparked public outrage and led to legal action against King and Pearson, with King confessing to everything – meaning Pearson got off scot-free.

In 1889, King was tried and convicted for neglect and cruelty, being sent to the gallows for her part in one of the darkest chapters in Edinburgh's history.

Thankfully, stories like this are as shocking as they are rare, and while Stockbridge has a darker side, it also has a haunted side. Perhaps the area's most notable haunting happened in one of its more affluent streets – Royal Circus. Royal Circus is a circle of Georgian townhouses designed by architect William Playfair and built between 1821 and 1829. The neoclassical-style houses, marked by Ionic columns and symmetry, reflect the architectural trends of the early nineteenth century. Each townhouse has a unique character, contributing to the overall charm of Royal Circus. Beyond its architectural significance, the site holds historical value as a residence for the city's elite during the nineteenth century. Circus Lane, adjacent to Royal Circus, served a practical purpose as stables for the affluent residents, embodying the functional aspect of the elite lifestyle in the nineteenth century. Today, Royal Circus stands as a preserved example of Georgian architecture in Edinburgh.

By the early 1970s, many of these formerly majestic properties had been transformed into self-contained units, still under the ownership and occupancy of those with the means. While most buildings had found new life, there was one lone property that stood vacant for a few years and was in the process of undergoing renovations to be repurposed into apartments. A local group of workmen, thrilled to secure the contract for the renovations, soon discovered why the property had stood empty for so long. As is often the case in such tales, the onset of the haunting was subtle, catching the men off guard. In the beginning, the disturbances were inconspicuous – tools mysteriously relocating, equipment stored overnight appearing in different corners of the property, or a hammer left on the floor during breaks mysteriously vanishing by the time the men returned. The men blamed each other, assuming the disappearances were an attempt at practical jokes. Yet their perception would soon shift as they came to the unsettling realisation that there was nothing funny about these peculiar occurrences.

The day that would eventually turn the men into believers began unremarkably. Upon reaching the property, they resumed their tasks from the previous day. Each man dispersed to a different section of the property to tackle their assigned duties for the day. As one of the men toiled near the foot of the main staircase, he caught the faint sound of what he interpreted as movement emanating from the floor above. Assuming it to be a colleague, he called out to find out who it was, only to be met with an eerie silence. After a brief pause, during which only the muffled sounds of hammering and power tools echoing from distant rooms could be heard, he concluded that he must have been mistaken, so carried on working.

After a few minutes, he felt a breeze blow past his face, and on looking up, he saw a dark-haired woman, in a long white dress, disappear through a doorway. Thinking someone was in the house with the workmen, he called out to her but again was met with complete silence, no one replied, and curiously, he couldn't hear the sound of movement. After a second or two of uncomfortable silence he took after the woman. Following the route she had taken, he was quickly in the room he'd seen her enter, but she was nowhere to be seen. He ran through another door, to an adjoining room – again, no one there.

Puzzled and concerned, he called out to his workmates, who soon came to see what the fuss was about. Explaining what he'd seen, they investigated the rest of the house, exploring every room on every floor, but their search turned up nothing – there was no sign of her. The men naturally came to the conclusion that the woman must have gotten into the property when a delivery was being made and had managed to get out without being noticed, so tried to put the events of the day out of their minds. However, this occurrence repeated itself on numerous subsequent occasions; a young woman with long, dark hair, clad in an old-fashioned white dress, was observed drifting around the property. The men were left bewildered, unable to track the woman down no matter how thoroughly they searched – how was she getting in, and how was she getting out? The men's confusion would soon give way to belief.

A few weeks after the mysterious woman's initial appearance, three of the workmen took a well-earned rest and enjoyed their lunch, unaware that a subtle chill was filling the air. The surroundings began to shift imperceptibly around them. The radio, once playing softly, now emitted nothing but white noise. The room darkened, and an unsettling silence crept in. Suddenly, the temperature dropped noticeably, prompting the workmen to exchange puzzled glances. Just as they were on the verge of dismissing this strange occurrence, the ghostly figure of the dark-haired woman slowly walked into the room, sending shivers down their spines. The men watched, mouths wide open, as the figure seemed to glide across the floor, towards a closed door on the other side of the room, without making a sound. Before reaching the door, the woman began to fade away, disappearing right before their eyes. Now there could be no doubt, they hadn't been tricked or outpaced by someone who'd snuck into the property, they had seen a ghost, the apparition of a young woman with long dark hair, wearing an old-fashioned white dress. The three men immediately downed tools and ran out of the property.

Overwhelmed by fear and unable to muster the courage to resume work, the distressed workmen sought solace from their union representative. Struck by the authenticity of their terror, the union rep, recognizing the need for unconventional intervention, reached out to a psychic they had consulted for a reading in the past. A few days later, the psychic arrived at the property, accompanied by the union rep, who provided moral support. The witnesses, paralyzed by dread, hesitated to re-enter the building and waited outside. Undertaking a thorough walkthrough of each room, the psychic claimed to establish a connection with the spirit of the long-deceased woman. Exiting the premises, she spoke with the anxious workmen. Assuring them that there was nothing to fear, the psychic conveyed that the apparition they had encountered was at peace and harboured no ill intentions. Following a discussion with the union rep, the workmen reluctantly agreed to return to their duties, albeit with stringent conditions – pairing up for work and a firm commitment to avoid solitary tasks. The lingering unease was palpable as they cautiously stepped back into the haunted building, their collective apprehension a constant companion. But they reported no further sightings or interactions with the dark-haired woman. The events that transpired at the haunted property left an ineffaceable mark on the workmen, their experience serving as a chilling reminder of the supernatural.

After the visit from the psychic and the union rep, calm returned, and there were no further sightings or encounters reported by those working on the renovations. It seemed as though the psychic's intervention had brought a sense of closure, and the spirit of the dark-haired woman had found peace. As for the identity of the spirit, local lore suggests that the apparition could be connected to the property's history, possibly a former resident or someone with a strong emotional tie to the place.

The specific details remain shrouded in mystery, but the psychic's assurance that the spirit meant no harm offered a semblance of comfort to those who had witnessed her ghostly presence. Over the years, residents of the converted property have not reported any encounters with the dark-haired woman. Whether she moved on or found solace in the resolution brought about by the psychic's visit remains a matter of speculation. It could also be possible that she still visits, with residents too fearful to report encounters with her.

The stories of the Royal Circus haunting remind us of Edinburgh's rich history, hidden beneath its elegant facades. Today, Stockbridge is a lively area with bars, markets, and eateries. Amidst its sandstone streets and vibrant community, it's easy to forget the unsettling events that once took place. Including these tales in my book shows that, despite its modern appeal, Stockbridge remains one of Edinburgh's most haunted areas.

CHAPTER 12
OLD CRAIG HOUSE, MORNINGSIDE

"Aw fur coat and nae knickers" – a phrase often used to describe the residents of Morningside – reflects the perception that while they may project an image of refinement and sophistication, the reality may not always match up.

Located in the south-west of Edinburgh, Morningside has a rich history dating back centuries. Once a rural area outside the city, Morningside began to flourish in the nineteenth century as Edinburgh's urban boundaries expanded. Formerly farmland, it gradually transformed into a sought-after residential suburb, attracting affluent residents seeking a quieter lifestyle away from the hustle and bustle of the city centre. The establishment of the Morningside Railway Station in 1884 further spurred growth and accessibility, facilitating the area's development.

Morningside, named for its location on the eastern slope, or "morning side", of the ancient Burgh Muir, now part of modern Edinburgh, has evolved into a vibrant community. Its streets feature a blend of Victorian and Edwardian architecture mixed with contemporary buildings. The area is known for its bustling high street, charming shops, and verdant green spaces, preserving its historical charm while offering modern amenities. Beneath its polished exterior, Morningside maintains an intriguing atmosphere where tradition and modernity intersect.

The area is also notable for its many street names with biblical references, such as Canaan Lane, Egypt Mews, Jordan Lane, and Nile Grove. The origins of these references remain uncertain, but one prevailing theory suggests a connection to Little Egypt Farm, once located between Braid Road and Blackford Hill. This farm may have been named after a settlement of Romanies who arrived in the area after being expelled from Edinburgh in 1540, with the term "gypsy" possibly derived from "Egyptian". In the Braid area, street names like Braid Road and Braidburn Terrace trace their origins to the estate of Sir Henry de Brade, a sheriff of Edinburgh in the twelfth century. The estate's name, in Gaelic, "bràghaid", signifies a throat or gorge, alluding to the deep cut in the Braid Burn near the present Braidburn Valley Park.

Having lived in Morningside at various points in my life, my own experiences colour my perception of this area's history. For several years, I resided on Jordan Lane and briefly in a top-floor flat in Morningside Park with my good friend Jennie. The flat, owned by Jennie's parents, became my home for a few months in the mid-'90s.

The flat was on the top floor – four flights up – and at the end of the stairwell. Inside, there was a long, L-shaped hallway. Jennie's room was first on the left and her parents' room on the right, followed by the living room. Turning to face the bathroom straight ahead, my room was on the left and the kitchen on the right.

Living there, I became deeply familiar with the unique charm and character of Morningside, experiencing firsthand the blend of history and modern life that defines this remarkable area.

In those days, I worked in a supermarket on the other side of the city. I remember one day, during my shift, being told there was a call for me, and when I answered, it was Jennie, panicked. She told me that she was in the kitchen and could hear someone walking around in the living room with the occasional banging noise. Given I was at least thirty minutes away, there wasn't much I could do, so I suggested taking a hammer or something hefty, then making a run past the living room (where the noises were coming from) and out the door, to find a neighbour and ask them to go back into the flat with them, which she did.

When she and the neighbour returned, they gingerly made their way into the living room. There, they found the stereo speakers, which were securely mounted on the walls, now on the floor. We never discovered how and why they came to be there, but used to freak each other out by saying it was "the Green Lady of Morningside".

And it's the Green Lady who features in our next story.

To the west of Morningside lies the area of Craiglockhart, an area rich in history and significance. Craiglockhart has long been known for its beautiful landscapes and its role in Edinburgh's development. Historically, it was home to the powerful Elphinstone family, who played a significant role in the area's history. The Elphinstones, a prominent Scottish family, owned large estates and held various titles over the centuries. Craiglockhart, with its rolling hills and scenic views, was one of their key properties. The family's influence is still evident in some of the area's place names and historical sites.

Craiglockhart is also notable for Craiglockhart Hydropathic, a former hydropathic institution established in the nineteenth century. During World War I, it served as a military hospital for officers suffering from shell shock. It was here that famous war poets Wilfred Owen and Siegfried Sassoon met and wrote some of their most impactful work.

Today, Craiglockhart is a thriving residential area, known for its mix of Victorian and Edwardian houses, modern developments, and green spaces like Craiglockhart Hill and Craiglockhart Nature Reserve. The area also features Craiglockhart Leisure and Tennis Centre, which offers various recreational facilities for the community.

Living close to such a historically rich area adds another layer of depth to the experience of residing in Morningside. The history of Craiglockhart, influenced by the Elphinstone family and its wartime significance, adds to the captivating fabric of Edinburgh's past and present.

In 1712, Sir Thomas Elphinstone, a former governor of Maryland in America, returned to Edinburgh and set up home in Craiglockhart in a large manor house near to Balcarres Street in Morningside. As a widower and father to John, Sir Thomas sensed that something was lacking in his life, a wife. On his travels, he'd met the much younger Betty Pittendale (forty years younger, in fact), and smitten with her, he pursued her endlessly.

There was a problem that Sir Thomas was not aware of; while in London, Betty had met and fallen for "Captain Jack Courage", as he was known at the time. She'd fallen head over heels in love, but when Captain Jack was posted to

Ireland, putting an end to their blossoming relationship, she eventually caved in to the constant pressure and agreed to marry Sir Thomas.

After a relatively short engagement period, the wedding day soon arrived, and with this, the tale takes a shocking and ultimately tragic twist. Lady Elphinstone, as Betty was now known, waited eagerly to meet Sir Thomas's young son John, who'd been overseas with the army. They met at the wedding reception, and to her horror, she realised that John was in fact her very own Captain Jack! She'd unintentionally married the father of the man she'd fallen in love with.

Given they now lived in the same house and were in each other's company often, passions between the young lovers intensified and ran high, with stolen and secret trysts threatening to expose their affection for each other. They both decided the correct course of action was for John to leave; his father, after all, was said to have a terrible temper, and there was genuine fear as to what would happen, to both of them, should he find out. Soon, the time came for John to return home, and he and Lady Elphinstone had one final meeting, where they said their goodbyes and parted with a final kiss. Unfortunately, Sir Thomas turned the corner at the precise time the couple shared their last embrace, a scuffle ensued, and he ran towards his young wife with his dagger in hand, plunging it into her heart, killing her instantly.

His anger immediately subsided, and upon realisation at what he had done, he begged his son to run him through with his sword, to which he refused. Instead, John picked up the body of his love and carried her to her room, placing her gently on her bed, still wearing her favourite green dress. Here, he left his father to mourn at the bedside of the young woman he'd just murdered. Upon daybreak, Sir Thomas was found to have died through the night, his body hunched over Lady Elphinstone's dead body, clutching her hand.

As you can imagine, this was too much for John, who couldn't stay in the house any longer, so rented the property out to a close friend, Colonel Lamington, whose family consisted of his wife and daughter. On moving in, they hired a governess to help raise their young daughter, and after only a couple of weeks in the property, the servants began to speak of seeing the governess walking around late at night, in a green dress. The governess denied all knowledge of this and chided the servants for telling tales.

One morning at breakfast, Mrs Lamington noticed excitement in one of the servants and asked why he was in such a state. He told her that as he was retiring for the evening, a woman had entered his chambers, dressed in green. He described her as being in great distress, wringing her hands "piteously" and looking to the bed as if hoping to see someone there. Eventually the apparition disappeared.

For several consecutive nights, like clockwork, the same mysterious occurrence repeated itself, striking on the hour each time. Convinced initially that these were merely practical jokes orchestrated by someone in the household, the colonel took measures to confront the perpetrator. He had a second bed brought into the room so that he could remain vigilant through the night and catch the culprit in the act.

Sure enough, as the clock struck the designated hour, the apparition of the Green Lady materialised once more. Mistaking her spectral presence for that of a living person, the colonel attempted to engage her in conversation. However, in a bewildering twist, the apparition vanished before his eyes, leaving him puzzled and unsettled by the inexplicable encounter.

An hour later, the ghostly figure of the Green Lady reappeared in a sudden rush, accompanied this time by her enraged husband. He thundered, "You have disgraced both yourself and me!" before delivering a shocking blow, stabbing her in the heart.

This happened so frequently that eventually the Lamingtons were forced to move out, and John returned with a mystic called Kalidosa, who was brought to help lay the spirits of the dead. Drawing the signs of the zodiac and recounting incantations, Kalidosa was successful in raising the spirits of the tragic couple.

"Why have you summoned us?" they said in unison.

Kalidosa replied, "You, the dead, are disturbing the living. Has something been done to anger you?"

Lady Elphinstone's spirit reportedly communicated that her husband's coffin, placed directly above hers in their shared vault, disturbed her. She requested her coffin be relocated, which was soon carried out, leading to the apparent end of the haunting of the Green Lady of Morningside. Years later, upon Betty's 'Captain Jack's' passing, he was interred beside her, reuniting the young lovers in the afterlife once more.

While the story goes that the hauntings have stopped with the relocation of Lady Elphinstone's coffin, I have an aunt who lives about a mile southeast of Craiglockhart, in an area known as Comiston. Her house is near Fairmilehead public park, a small green space lined with large trees that were once part of the Elphinstone estate. The park, though modest now, still holds echoes of its grand past.

She told me recently that reports continue of sightings of a lady in an eighteenth-century green dress, wandering among the trees of Fairmilehead Park. Local legend says she is the ghost of a heartbroken woman, forever searching for her lost love. People say her presence is marked by an overwhelming sense of sadness. Those who claim to have seen her describe a figure in a long, flowing dress, moving silently through the park. Could this phantom be Lady Elphinstone, eternally trapped in a sorrowful quest through the tranquil glades of Fairmilehead Park?

I have included this often-overlooked story in the book to preserve the poignant tale of Lady Elphinstone, ensuring her story of enduring love and heartbreak remains part of our shared history.

CHAPTER 13
ROTHESAY PLACE

THE NEXT STAGE in the expansion of Edinburgh was the building of the area known as the West End.

The West End of Edinburgh has a rich and varied history, characterised by its development in the nineteenth century as an extension of the New Town and its association with the city's economic and cultural growth.

Before development began, the land was primarily rural and agricultural. Rolling hills and open fields stretched across the area, interspersed with small villages and country estates. This countryside landscape provided a stark contrast to the densely packed and vertically developed Old Town of Edinburgh, which was confined within its mediaeval city walls. The fertile land, enriched by streams and rivers like the Water of Leith, supported a variety of agricultural activities, including farming and grazing, which sustained Edinburgh and the local communities with its produce. However, marshy areas and wetlands also dotted the landscape, contributing to the ecosystem and providing natural habitats. Over time, as Edinburgh's population surged and the demand for residential space outside the congested Old Town increased, the quiet rural character of the pre-West End era gradually gave way to urbanisation. Drainage and development projects were undertaken to reclaim and transform these marshy lands, paving the way for the emergence of the vibrant West End as we know it today.

The West End began to develop in the early nineteenth century, following the success of the New Town's Georgian architecture. The area was designed to accommodate Edinburgh's growing population and increasing wealth, meeting the demand for more spacious and elegant residences. The architecture in the West End is predominantly Georgian and Victorian, with grand townhouses, terraces, and crescents. Notable architects like John Lessels contributed to the area's distinctive style.

As the city expanded, the West End became an important commercial district. The establishment of Haymarket Station in 1842 made it a key transportation hub, further boosting its economic significance. The area attracted numerous businesses, including financial institutions and law firms, establishing it as a significant business quarter.

The West End is home to several cultural landmarks, including the Scottish National Gallery of Modern Art and the Usher Hall, a premier concert venue opened in 1914. Throughout the nineteenth and early twentieth centuries, the West End became known for its vibrant social scene, with numerous clubs, restaurants, and theatres.

In recent decades, the West End has seen significant urban renewal and modernization efforts. Historic buildings have been preserved and repurposed for contemporary use, blending the area's rich history with modern amenities. Today, the West End remains one of Edinburgh's most desirable residential areas, known for its elegant architecture, proximity to the city centre, and a mix of high-end shops, cafes, and restaurants.

St Mary's Cathedral, an imposing Gothic Revival cathedral completed in 1879, is a key landmark in the West End. While technically a separate area, Dean Village is often associated with the West End due to its proximity. This historic milling village has become a picturesque residential area and one of Edinburgh's most "instagrammed" locations.

While the area is now a haven for tourists, its past hasn't always been so serene. In 1974, the first official residents began moving into the flats at West Mill, but perhaps they were not the only souls already residing there. One new resident reported seeing a white figure of a woman standing in mid-stream below the weir just before midnight shortly after moving in. Is it possible that the apparition they saw was the spirit of someone who had tragically drowned there? The famous Dean Bridge, spanning the Water of Leith and built in 1831 by Thomas Telford, has earned the moniker "the bridge of sighs" due to the number of tragic incidents that have occurred there. In around 1880, a sailor, heartbroken after being spurned by the woman he loved, tragically took his own life at this location. In commemoration, a statue known as *The Little Sailor Boy* was erected, depicting him gazing up at the bridge with a poignant expression of deep contemplation.

In 1958, the spacious residence of number 5 Rothesay Place found itself under the ownership of the Van Horne family, a young couple with dreams of settling into their new home. Little did they know that their lives would soon take a chilling turn.

Until that fateful year, the Van Hornes had enjoyed a sense of normalcy within their abode; life was as you would expect for a young family in post-war Edinburgh. However, their prosperity and tranquillity was abruptly shattered when they acquired a set of furniture from the estate of a recently deceased local resident – a pipe-smoking sailor, as rumour had it. This seemingly innocuous purchase would unknowingly invite an otherworldly presence into their midst.

As the Van Horne family settled the sailor's furnishings into their home, a series of peculiar, poltergeist-like occurrences began to unfold. Mysterious noises echoed through the halls at night, accompanied by inexplicable drafts and unexplained shadows flickering in the corners of rooms. The scent of pipe tobacco wafted through the air, lingering long after the last ember had faded away.

Soon, the Van Hornes found themselves confronted with more tangible manifestations of the supernatural. Objects would inexplicably move from their designated places, and doors would creak open of their own accord. Disturbed and bewildered, the family could not shake the feeling of being watched, as if an unseen presence lurked just beyond their line of sight. In July of that year, things took a very unusual turn.

Despite their efforts to rationalise or dispel the disturbances, the Van Horne family could not shake the feeling that their home was no longer theirs alone. With each passing day, the spectral presence seemed to grow bolder, its unseen grip tightening around the hearts of those who dared to cross its threshold.

In the midst of the Van Hornes' bewildering ordeal, they soon reported a peculiar phenomenon within their home. A mysterious ball of light, affectionately dubbed "Tinkerbell" by the startled residents, was observed flitting about the rooms and corridors in the property, its ethereal glow casting an haunting ambiance over the household.

However, the strangeness did not end there. In September of the same year, witnesses were stunned to encounter what appeared to be what was described as a "gnome" within the confines of the Van Horne residence. Clad in red trousers and a brown jacket – an unusual sartorial choice indeed – the enigmatic apparition, affectionately dubbed "Gnomey" by those who saw it, stood at a mere thirty centimetres in height, defying all conventional explanation.

Although small in size, "Gnomey" soon became a common presence in the Van Hornes' residence, his mysterious appearances adding to the uncertainty and intrigue surrounding the household. In addition to these ghostly sightings, the house remained filled with inexplicable noises, and objects appeared to move autonomously.

As the months turned into years, the paranormal activity persisted, and sightings of the foot-tall Gnomey and the flickering Tinkerbell persisted. However, come the early 1960s, the disturbances inexplicably ceased, leaving a lingering sense of mystery and unanswered questions in their wake.

As whispers of the haunting circulated throughout Rothesay Place, neighbours exchanged nervous glances and shared tales of the inexplicable phenomena. The once warm and inviting atmosphere of the neighbourhood now carried an unsettling pall, with the Van Horne residence at its epicentre.

The unusual haunting of number 5 Rothesay Place serves as a chilling reminder of the thin boundary between the living and the unknown. Even in the most mundane of locales, the echoes of the past can linger, spinning tales of tragedy and mystery that resist fading into obscurity.

The inclusion of such an astonishing account in this book is vital, especially considering the area's transformation into an upmarket, respectable neighbourhood with numerous hotels and surrounded by embassies.

It's rare to encounter a poltergeist case involving an apparition, let alone the apparition of a foot-tall "gnome". The only other example that comes to mind featuring such an enigmatic element is the curious case of Gef, the talking mongoose from the Isle of Man in the 1930s. Gef was purportedly a talking mongoose who communicated with a family living on the Isle of Man, exhibiting extraordinary intelligence and supernatural abilities, which has fascinated paranormal enthusiasts for decades.

As the area moves away from being a residential area to a commercial and diplomatic hub, the tales of its haunted past risk fading into obscurity amidst the focus on modern amenities and prestige, and unique tales like the one from Rothesay Place are at risk of being lost. Therefore, it's essential to preserve such encounters to safeguard the rich history of Edinburgh's haunted past.

CHAPTER 14
CLOSING

While Edinburgh's Old Town is a mecca for tourism, a short ten-minute walk north of the Royal Mile, across the famous Princes Street, takes you to the New Town. Despite its relatively brief existence by Edinburgh standards, the New Town is as equally rich in history and heritage as the Old Town. A stroll around its wide, airy streets with grand sandstone buildings is just as enjoyable and educational as exploring the bustling confines of Edinburgh's more ancient streets. While the atmospheric Royal Mile is well known as a haunted location, the elegance of the New Town doesn't immediately conjure up images of haunted houses and women in white, but it is an incredibly haunted area.

The New Town and wider Edinburgh's supernatural activity covers almost the full paranormal spectrum, including reports of ghostly footsteps echoing through Georgian homes and mysterious figures appearing in the grand townhouses. The spirits of those who once walked these streets seem to endure, adding an unexpected layer of fascination and enchantment to the area's stately charm.

Travel further afield, and you'll find that the once separate ancient villages, such as Corstorphine and Stockbridge, now part of Edinburgh, each have their own paranormal tales. The wider Edinburgh area is just as historic and mysterious as the city's ancient roots. Perhaps it's not just the buildings that hold the energy and memories of the past, but the land itself that makes Edinburgh one of the most haunted places in the world. This land, steeped in centuries of conflicts, bloodshed and emotions, might be the true repository of the city's haunted legacy.

The New Town brought hope to some, but its grandeur couldn't conceal the hardships faced by many. While living standards improved for a fortunate few, the majority continued to endure challenges reminiscent of those in Edinburgh's Old Town. This stark reality is exemplified by the tragic tale of the Stockbridge "baby farm", a poignant reminder that progress was uneven and that deep-seated social issues persisted despite the era's aspirations for modernity and prosperity. Could the lingering spectres of Edinburgh's past, embedded in the very fabric of its landscapes and witnessed in the tales of its haunted locales, be a testament to the enduring impact of history's trials and tribulations on the city's collective memory?

In closing, our journey beyond the Old Town has revealed a wealth of unreported and overlooked ghost stories that add depth to Edinburgh's haunted heritage. These testimonies, though less well known, are no less chilling or significant. They remind us that history's echoes linger in every corner of this ancient city, waiting to be discovered by those willing to look beyond the familiar and convenient.

As you walk the streets of Edinburgh, may you be inspired to uncover the hidden stories that lie in the shadows, adding your own chapters to the city's ghostly lore. Explore the grand avenues of the New Town, the winding paths of old villages, and let the whispers of the past guide you to uncover the mysteries that make Edinburgh a truly haunted city.

PART THREE
SHADOWS BEYOND EDINBURGH
HAUNTINGS ACROSS SCOTLAND

In our final chapter, we cast our gaze beyond the boundaries of the capital city into the misty moors, ancient castles, and remote villages that dot the Scottish landscape. From the atmospheric ruins of forgotten abbeys to the windswept shores of distant islands, Scotland's haunted history extends far beyond the city limits of Edinburgh.

My love for a good ghost story is almost eclipsed by my passion and enthusiasm for exploring this truly magnificent country. My friends often joke that Visit Scotland should sponsor me, as I speak so highly and with such enthusiasm about the land of my birth.

When I'm not immersed in a ghost story, I can often be found wandering through the glens and forests of Scotland. There's nothing that beats the sensation of being surrounded by a forest of old Scots pines while listening to the waters of one of our thirty thousand lochs gently lapping against the shore.

My go-to places are usually around Perth, Blair Atholl, and Pitlochry, especially for shorter trips. Blair Atholl in particular is a must if you want to experience the picture-postcard beauty of Scotland. It's located on the southern edge of the Cairngorm national park and is surrounded by some particularly stunning hillwalking country. There are the peaks of Beinn a' Ghlò, Càrn a' Chlamain, and Beinn Dearg, as well as secluded valleys like Glen Tilt and Glen Banvie (my personal favourite). Towards the historic white walls of Blair Castle, you'll also find the Falls of Bruar hidden away amidst the enchanting woodland of the Atholl Estate. The surrounding forest, with its Scots pines, redwoods planted from seeds brought over from America, and moss-covered rocks, adds a mystical charm to this scenic Highland destination.

However, if I have more time, I often venture further north or west, frequently exploring sections of the NC500 – a route steeped in history and ghostly mystery, which I covered in depth in my first book, *Ghostly Tales of the NC500*.

In this section, we journey across the length and breadth of the country, uncovering accounts of restless spirits, spectral apparitions, and ghostly phenomena that continue to haunt this majestic land.

At Liarn Farm on the banks of Kinloch Rannoch, in the shadow of the mighty and mysterious Schiehallion, three long-forgotten stories close to my heart emerge from this remote and rugged landscape, each more chilling than the last. The farm's isolation and stark beauty serve as the perfect backdrop for ghostly encounters that defy explanation.

The once grand Ballechin House, at one point reported to be the most haunted house in Scotland, stands as a testament to the area's historic and eerie past. Its mysterious history is filled with unsettling occurrences that have left a lasting impression on all who have crossed its threshold. The house's dark corridors and shadowy rooms have witnessed countless unexplained events that once captivated Victorian Britain and made headlines all over the world.

In Bearsden, a suburb of Glasgow, the spectres of the past make their presence known in ways that defy logic. This seemingly quiet area is home to previously undocumented stories of hauntings that disturb the peace of its residents, adding a new chapter to Scotland's incredible history of paranormal experiences.

From the Highlands to the Lowlands, from the Borders to the Inner Hebrides, join us as we explore the supernatural echoes that lurk in the dark corners of Scotland's storied past.

These encounters remind us that every part of Scotland, no matter how remote, has a tale to tell, and the past is always closer than we think.

CHAPTER 15
BALLECHIN HOUSE, GRANDTULLY

Scotland's history is a complex interweaving of shifting capitals and political dynamics. While Edinburgh is the contemporary capital, it hasn't always held this esteemed position. Centuries ago, the heart of Scottish power beat in the region of Perth, with the seat of authority shifting between Scone and Perth during the early mediaeval periods. This rotation was a reflection of Scotland's evolving political landscape, where power was centred in the monarch's chosen residence. However, the chapter that solidified Edinburgh's status as the enduring capital began in 1437. It was during this pivotal moment that power moved from Perth to the more defensible Edinburgh. This marked a significant departure from the previous practice of moving the capital based on royal preference.

Before this transformative shift, Edinburgh occupied a more modest role in Scotland's political theatre as a royal residence. Its transformation into a permanent capital heralded an era of stability and growth, setting the stage for Edinburgh to become the vibrant and influential capital that we know today. This historical journey exemplifies the ever-evolving nature of Scotland's identity, as reflected in its capital cities throughout the ages.

Before Edinburgh held power, the capital moved from place to place, and during the first war of Independence, Edward Longshanks established the ancient city of Perth as his capital when he held power between 1296 and 1312. Prior to this, Scone was the seat of power, also the site where Scotland's monarchs were crowned. Perth was the last capital of Scotland before moving to Edinburgh between 1406 and 1437, and it was the assassination of King James I in Perth that finally led to Edinburgh being established as the nation's capital.

The assassination of King James I of Scotland in 1437 remains a chilling chapter in Scottish history. A group of disaffected nobles, led by Sir Robert Graham, plotted against the king, who had sought to assert royal authority and curb the power of the nobility. On a fateful night in February, they breached the walls of the Carthusian Priory in Perth, where James I was residing. Bursting into his chamber, they subjected the monarch to a brutal and fatal attack, ending his life with multiple stab wounds. This regicide plunged Scotland into a period of political turmoil, as James's young son, who would become James II, was left to ascend the throne while the nobles jockeyed for power.

Along with political and historical intrigue, Perth also has a long history of the less tangible type. Stories of fairies, water spirits, and hauntings have persisted throughout this region for as long as people have lived there. Perhaps the most compelling account of a haunting took place in the nineteenth century in Ballechin House, near Grandtully around twenty-five miles northwest of Perth. Ballechin House was originally constructed in the early nineteenth century, around 1806. It was designed by the renowned Scottish architect Robert Smirke for the Steuart family, who'd built and owned the manor house on the property prior. The house was built in the period's Georgian style and set in some beautiful gardens; however, in the mid-twentieth century, the house was abandoned and fell into a state of disrepair.

In this story, we explore the story of Ballechin House, once dubbed "the most haunted house in Scotland". Before the house sadly fell into ruin, in 1834 Major Robert Steuart inherited Ballechin, and while serving abroad in the Indian Army, he rented the sprawling manor. After dutifully serving in India, where he earned a battle scar in the form of a leg wound that forever altered his stride, the major continued to dedicate himself to his military career for an additional twenty-five years. Upon his well-deserved retirement, he made the return to his cherished ancestral residence, Ballechin House. His time in India had forever altered his outlook on life; he became a lover of dogs and brought many home with him to Scotland. He also became a believer in reincarnation, specifically the ability of the human soul to inhabit a non-human body after death. His belief in this was so strong that his wish upon his death was that his spirit would return to occupy his favourite dog, a beautiful black spaniel.

The major led a rather solitary life during his later years, with his sole companion being a young servant named Sarah. Unfortunately, tragedy struck in 1873 when Sarah passed away suddenly and under mysterious circumstances, leaving the major to live out his days in solitude until his own passing in 1876 at the age of seventy. As he had never married, Ballechin House eventually passed into the ownership of the major's nephew, John. However, John strongly opposed his uncle's dying wish of having his faithful dog continue to live in the house, and he took a drastic and disturbing measure. Prior to moving in with his family, John ordered the execution of his uncle's loyal companions. This cruel act would later prove to be the catalyst for the haunting that would plague Ballechin House.

Shortly after this horrifying incident, the manor house was plunged into a series of bizarre occurrences. Unexplained knocking and rapping sounds reverberated through the walls and empty rooms, even after thorough investigations confirmed no one else was present. To make matters spookier, the dead of night often resonated with the echoes of heated arguments despite every member of the household having been accounted for. On occasion, the terrifying sound of an explosion was heard echoing through the house, terrifying everyone who heard it. John's wife reported being in what was the major's study one day when she encountered the overpowering and unmistakable smell of dogs, and at the same time, she felt a dog brush against her leg as if walking by her. Events became so frequent and so unsettling that the governess and maids wouldn't stay in the house and had to work in pairs.

John was even compelled to build a new wing onto the house to move his family into, as they also struggled to stay in the main house. The heart of the haunting centred on the main bedroom, the very room where Sarah, the major's sole companion, had met her mysterious and untimely demise. In 1895, John found himself in this very room, engrossed in a telephone conversation with his agent about an upcoming trip to London. However, their exchange was abruptly halted by three thunderous and inexplicable bangs that seemed to resonate from some otherworldly source. Soon John departed for London, and shortly after his arrival, tragedy struck. As he made his way from Kings Cross Station, crossing a busy street, a passing cab collided with him, killing him instantly. Those aware of the eerie incident with the bangs couldn't help but view it as an ominous harbinger of doom.

During the Victorian era, Spiritualism had gained immense popularity throughout Britain, and it wasn't long before the spine-tingling tales of Ballechin House permeated the collective consciousness of the time. The house swiftly garnered notoriety for the series of haunting incidents that unfolded within its walls. Visitors and locals alike couldn't resist discussing the mysterious occurrences, which added a layer of fascination and apprehension to this already enigmatic residence. As stories of apparitions, inexplicable sounds, and unsettling events continued to circulate, Ballechin House became an emblem of the era's fascination with the supernatural, cementing its place in the annals of Victorian ghost lore. In 1892, Father Hayden, a Jesuit priest, was invited to spend two nights in the old manor house while journeying through Scotland.

After a pleasant evening of dinner and company upon his arrival, he retired to his bed late that night, expecting a peaceful rest. However, his slumber was abruptly shattered by a cacophony of unsettling sounds – animal-like noises, mournful wails, and inexplicable knocks reverberating through the walls. The disturbances left him so unnerved that at the break of dawn, he promptly requested a room change, eager to distance himself from the disquieting commotion. The priest's experiences with Ballechin House were not limited to his initial encounter. A year later, his path serendipitously crossed with a former governess who had served within the property for a twelve-year period. Coincidentally, this former employee had also chosen to stay in the very same two rooms that had been the epicentre of the unsettling events that had troubled the priest during his earlier visit.

As she shared her own experiences, a pattern of eerily similar phenomena began to emerge. She too recounted hearing those same inexplicable noises – the sounds of animals, mournful wails, and mysterious knocks echoing through the ancient walls. Her experiences scared her so much that she soon ended her employment with the family and soon left the area, moving far away from Ballechin House. Four years later, a hopeful young family eagerly signed the rental agreement for Ballechin House, imagining it as their tranquil abode for the upcoming year. Little did they know that their stay would soon be marred by a resurgence of the poltergeist-like activity that had tormented previous occupants.

Soon after moving in, the family found themselves immersed in the unsettling world of Ballechin House. The most common paranormal occurrences took the form of disconcerting noises: mysterious knocks, thumps, and echoing footsteps reverberated through the ancient halls, becoming an almost daily ordeal. However, one night would etch the most terrifying memory into their minds. As the parents slumbered peacefully in their bed, a tremendous thud jolted them awake. To their sheer horror, their bedsheets were forcibly ripped off the bed by unseen hands, an experience that sent shivers down their spines. Regularly a white misty form would be witnessed moving silently from room to room. Yet the most chilling encounter occurred when their children reported witnessing the apparition of a man.

This phantom figure stood silently, casting an eerie gaze upon them from the shadowy corner of their bedroom. This was the straw that broke the camel's back. Overwhelmed by the relentless onslaught of unexplained events, the family chose to vacate the premises. Their stay in Ballechin was abruptly cut short after enduring just eleven harrowing weeks within its haunted confines. A year later, in 1897, Ballechin House became the focal point of an extensive investigation orchestrated by John Crichton-Stuart, the 3rd Marquess of Bute, in collaboration with paranormal researchers from the Society for Psychical Research (SPR). This stately residence had earned itself the reputation as "the Most Haunted House in Scotland", drawing unsettling parallels with the Borley Rectory haunting, even including claims of a ghostly nun's apparition.

Among the investigators, the team featured Colonel Lemesurier Taylor and the infamous medium Ada Goodrich Freer, sometimes more colourfully referred to as Miss X. The investigation invited a total of thirty-five guests, who all stayed at least one night in the house. None of the guests were given prior knowledge of the haunting and were invited to record any unusual activity they may experience during their time in the stately home. As with the previous encounters, guests often reported audible phenomena as the main experience. With sighs, raps, footsteps, and even the sound of what someone took to be a priest praying out loud. A disembodied hand was seen at the foot of one guest's bed, holding a crucifix. Perhaps, most unusually, a figure described as a "hunchback" was witnessed slowly walking up the main staircase.

A spectral black spaniel was seen, and noises, like that of dog tails wagging and striking a door, were also witnessed. One evening, as a guest slept, she was woken by the sound of a ghostly hound whimpering in her room. When she lit a candle, she saw the famous spaniel's disembodied paws perched on top of her dresser. During the investigation, the staff were also not immune to the ghostly goings-on, and a maid reported seeing the top half of the apparition of a woman seemingly suspended in mid-air. Ouija board sessions formed a central part of the investigation, and it was during one evening's gathering that the investigators received a mysterious message. They were instructed to venture to a nearby glen later that very night. Intrigued and somewhat apprehensive, they complied with the otherworldly directive. As they arrived at the remote glen, an unsettling sight unfolded before their eyes.

A haunting figure, unmistakably resembling a nun, was slowly traversing the landscape. The apparition's appearance was striking; she appeared youthful, her long, dark hair cascading like a shroud. Onlookers reported that she often exhibited signs of distress, with tears streaming down her pale countenance. At times, she appeared to engage in silent discourse with an unseen presence, heightening the mystique surrounding her. This recurring encounter with the sorrowful apparition intensified the sense of intrigue and unease among the investigators. They were left grappling with an unsettling question: who was this ghostly nun, and what lingering connection did she hold with the enigmatic history of Ballechin House?

The findings of their inquiry culminated in the publication of "The Alleged Haunting of B—— House" in 1899, which was serialised in the *Times*. This work contained a comprehensive journal meticulously maintained by Freer, documenting the supernatural phenomena they encountered. As the years passed, Ballechin House fell into disuse and disrepair, ultimately becoming uninhabited by 1932. Tragedy struck in 1963 when a devastating fire ravaged the majority of the structure. Sadly, this blaze consumed not only architectural splendours but also priceless artwork and furniture amassed over generations by the Steuart family. Although largely forgotten about now, in the realm of Scotland's haunted history, Ballechin earned its reputation as "Scotland's Most Haunted House" for undeniable reasons.

Almost every type of paranormal phenomenon was recorded there, by multiple independent witnesses, throughout its short existence. I can't help but wonder if a character like Harry Price had been around at the time of the hauntings, would Ballechin be more prominent in modern culture, as Borley Rectory is today. Perhaps the most unsettling aspect of this haunting is the enigma surrounding its origin – the haunting may very well have been instigated by the audacious request of the former owner, Major Steuart. His dying wish that he be reincarnated into his favourite spaniel and the cruel slaughter of his beloved hounds by his nephew may very well have been the violent catalyst for the events unfolded. Or could it have been the untimely and mysterious death of Sarah, the major's only companion?

Whatever the trigger, Ballechin House remains a place where the past and the paranormal intertwine, and its reputation as Scotland's Most Haunted House continues to capture the imaginations of those who dare to delve into its haunting mysteries.

Scotland's history is a complex interplay of politics, culture, and mystery. Edinburgh's rise as the capital city marked a significant shift, but before its ascendancy, other regions, like Perth, held sway. Ballechin House, once known as "Scotland's Most Haunted House", has since faded from memory despite its notoriety, much like other tales lost to time.

By including its story here, I hope to revive its chilling history and shed light on its forgotten mysteries. To me, Ballechin

House represents more than paranormal encounters; it embodies our enduring fascination with the unknown.

As I conclude this exploration, I carry with me a deeper appreciation for Scotland's haunted past and a renewed curiosity for the tales yet to be unearthed, leaving me to wonder, what other tales like Ballechin are out there?

CHAPTER 16
BEARSDEN, GLASGOW

In 2023 I was contacted by a lady from Glasgow who told me about an old Georgian house in the suburb of Bearsden with one of the creepiest hauntings I've ever heard.

She has asked for anonymity, so we will refer to her as Martha, and I won't mention the address of the haunting other than it's in Bearsden, which lies in the north-west outskirts of Glasgow.

The land that Bearsden now occupies has had huge historical significance throughout much of Scotland's history. The area's heritage can be traced back to Roman times when it held a strategic location situated along the Antonine Wall, the northernmost frontier of the Roman Empire in Britain, at a time when Scotland was known as Caledonia. Roman artefacts, including remnants of a military bathhouse, have been unearthed in Bearsden. However, it was during the nineteenth century that Bearsden began to evolve into a sought-after residential area. With the advent of the railway in the mid-1800s, the district became more accessible, attracting wealthy Glaswegians looking to escape the city's urban hustle and bustle. This led to the development of grand Victorian and Edwardian villas, which still grace the streets today.

Bearsden's growth continued throughout the twentieth century, becoming a thriving commuter suburb with excellent amenities and educational facilities, and it's Bearsden that this story focuses on.

As mentioned, the house that features in this encounter is from the late Georgian period, which ranged from 1760 to 1830. The house is an elegant and spacious dwelling, reflective of the architectural trends of the late eighteenth and early nineteenth centuries. The exterior features a symmetrical and proportioned facade with large, rectangular windows, and as with most Georgian houses, it has a rectangular structure with a central hallway leading from the front door to the back of the house. The rooms on each side of the hallway are spacious and well-lit, with high ceilings. The ground floor was the typical Georgian design that initially would have included a formal dining and drawing room, while the upper floors consisted of bedrooms and an attic space. Over the years, the large house was split into two homes.

Around ten years ago, Martha moved into one of the first-floor rooms that she rented from the owner, a friend of hers we'll call Rose. The room suited Martha perfectly, just like the house itself – grand, spacious, situated in a safe and tranquil neighbourhood. Its proximity to Glasgow allowed for a convenient commute, yet it was far enough away to provide a peaceful retreat from the stresses of work. However, this haven of tranquillity would soon become a place of fear and dread.

Shortly after Martha's move, she couldn't escape the realisation that this home was unlike any other she had lived in before, despite sharing it with one of her closest friends. The atmosphere consistently felt oppressive and unwelcoming, leaving her with a distinct impression that something about the house was different. In moments of solitude, Martha began hearing peculiar noises emanating from the attic – distinct, heavy footsteps, reminiscent of someone wearing old-fashioned hobnail boots, walking across what she knew to be an empty room. These unsettling sounds occurred at various times, disrupting her studies during the day and even waking her in the dead of night. Despite thorough investigations, the room was always found empty. Initially, Martha dismissed these sounds as mere echoes in an old house, attributing them to the acoustics of the chimneys. However, the persistence of these footsteps, particularly when standing near the entrance to the attic, forced her to reconsider.

On one occasion she was about to enter her room when she heard the noises again. Placing her ear to the attic door, Martha felt the vibrations and sounds, convincing her that what she was hearing couldn't be explained away as mere acoustics. Convinced that someone was wandering around the unoccupied attic, Martha cautiously opened the door, half-expecting to find her friend Rose. To her surprise, the room was still, quiet, and the footsteps had stopped. The room was empty; there was no one there, well…no one visible. In response to these experiences, Martha took to locking her room door whenever she was alone, opting to ignore the unsettling footsteps that echoed through the silent house.

The attic room wouldn't remain empty for long; being a large spacious room, it was the perfect size for an extra bedroom; and soon one of Martha's friends, whom we'll call Peter, rented it out. As with Martha, Peter quickly came to the realisation that this house wasn't like other houses. He often also heard footsteps walking across the attic floor, with no visible agent present. Occasionally he, out of the corner of his eye, glimpsed what he thought to be a dog in the attic, pacing back and forth around the room, but no one in the house owned a dog, so he put it down to an overactive imagination or a trick of the light. However, one night, he awoke in a panic, feeling an overwhelming sensation of breathlessness. As he regained his senses, he discerned the silhouette of a sizable dark dog sprawled across his chest, its weight pressing down and impeding his ability to draw in a full breath. Panicked, he attempted to push the dog off his chest, but he was met with no resistance; his arms had passed straight through whatever had sat on him. After a few seconds, the oppressive weight lifted, and Peter took in a large gasp of air. Whatever was stopping him breathing had disappeared.

Martha often had her mother, Linda, travel to visit her, sleeping in the spare room when she'd stay. Linda would travel up from England and, to make the most of her time with Martha, would stay for several days at a time. During one trip, Linda planned to stay over for a couple of nights, and she and Martha planned to make the most of their time together.

After a day visiting some of the fine galleries and museums in Glasgow, they returned to Bearsden, and Linda, tired from a busy day, retired for the night. Morning came, and Martha, being an early bird, knocked on Linda's door to wake her for breakfast. "How did you sleep?" she asked.

"I slept fine except for being woken by that angry girl at the window."

Confused, Martha asked Linda to repeat what she'd said. Linda described being woken in the middle of the night by the feeling that she was being watched. Although the room was dark, the curtains were open, and there was a dim light illuminating the room from the outside street light. Her attention was drawn to the large window opposite her bed. As her eyes adjusted to the dark, she started to make out the outline of someone standing outside the window. Thinking she must be still half asleep and imagining something that wasn't there – after all, she was in a room on the first floor and seeing someone outside her window – she sat up and rubbed her eyes, but looking again, she could see the figure was still there.

What Linda described to Martha was that she could see the upper half of a young, brown-haired woman. A woman with a wretched, twisted appearance. Her hair and face were filthy; her clothes looked how Linda imagined the clothes of someone who worked in a Victorian workhouse to be. Linda's confusion was soon replaced by terror when her gaze fell on the young girl's face. She was staring back, directly at Linda. There was a look of pure rage on this young woman's face, her lips were pulled back, and sharp, dirty teeth were visible. The woman also appeared to be lashing out at Linda, as if she was trying to scratch her. Linda weakly called out, "Hello," only for the figure at the window to vanish, blending seamlessly into the obscurity of the night. Linda, a rationally minded person, assumed that what she had witnessed was the product of a dream, and both she and Martha put the incident out of their minds. For now…

After the first night's events, Linda opted to sleep on the couch in the living room. On the mantelpiece was an urn that contained the ashes of Rose's mother, given pride of place above the fire. That night, Linda awoke to an unusual glow from the urn, as if it were red hot. Thinking it was morning and the sun was beaming through a gap in the curtain, she got up to close them but then realised it was still dark outside. She turned to look at the urn, which was still glowing but now dimming before returning to normal.

Two days later, one of Martha's friends came to visit, and he too slept over in the spare room. In the morning, Martha again asked how he slept.

"Fine until that woman woke me up walking across the room."

When Martha asked him to explain what he'd seen, he told her how he'd been woken up in the middle of the night and witnessed a young woman walking across his room before disappearing through the door. He described the woman as having brown hair and wearing clothes reminiscent of those someone from a workhouse would have worn a couple of hundred years earlier. The same outfit as the woman who'd appeared at the window had worn.

I want to express my gratitude to her for reaching out and sharing what happened. The apparitions and mysterious sounds in this tale unveil the history of this unique residence and prompt us to question why the hauntings persist. After sharing this story on my Eerie Edinburgh YouTube channel, one viewer left a striking comment suggesting that the appearance of the young woman may be attributed to syphilis, specifically Hutchinson's teeth. Hutchinson's teeth are a dental anomaly associated with congenital syphilis, transmitted from mother to child during pregnancy. They manifest as notched, peg-shaped incisors and are part of Hutchinson's triad, which also includes interstitial keratitis and deafness.

Could the woman seen have suffered from this condition, her spectral appearance marked by congenital syphilis?

I included this story in my book about unreported and overlooked ghost stories because it's a true ghost story, a fascinating and creepy account that sheds light on a haunting that might otherwise go unreported, and to top it all off, it's genuinely one of the most spine-tingling accounts I've heard to date.

CHAPTER 17
LIARN FARM, LOCH RANNOCH

SOME OF MY fondest childhood memories revolve around the weeks spent on summer holidays in Pitlochry, Perthshire – often hailed as the heart of Scotland. Its picturesque landscapes, including the majestic Munros, serene glens, meandering rivers, and dense forests, along with charmingly named places like Enochdu and Killiecrankie, epitomise the essence of Scotland. Adding to its allure is a rich historical significance, with Perth playing a central role in Scottish history for centuries.

My mother shared a profound love for the region, often expressing her desire to live there someday. When her last ties to Edinburgh (me) were severed, she seized the opportunity to fulfil her dream. Together with my dad, they made the decision to relocate to Loch Tay, then on to the beautiful shores of Loch Rannoch, situated on the outskirts of the renowned Rannoch Moor and within sight of the iconic mountain Schiehallion.

Kinloch Rannoch, the nearest town some six miles away from where my mother eventually settled, serves as a gateway to outdoor adventures such as hiking, fishing, and wildlife spotting. Schiehallion offers panoramic views of the surrounding countryside, while Loch Rannoch provides a serene setting for leisurely walks and boat trips. Rannoch is an area steeped in mystery and legend, with the 1,083-metre-high mountain Schiehallion at its heart.

"Schiehallion", a Gaelic word roughly translating to "Fairy Hill of the Caledonians" or "Hill of the Fairies", hints at the reverence ancient Celts once held for it. According to local legends, Schiehallion was believed to be a sacred mountain, inhabited by fairies or spirits known as "Sidhe", who were considered guardians of the land.

Legend has it that within Schiehallion lies a cave or series of caves that cut straight through the mountain. Upon venturing into these caverns, one encounters a peculiar phenomenon: a door swiftly materialises behind the explorer, sealing off any retreat.

On the mountain's southwest flank lies Tom a Mhorair, known as the Giant's Cave. Its entrance, spanning three to four metres in width, leads into sheltered darkness, earning it an age-old reputation as a portal to the underworld.

To the west lies Creag-na-h-Earra, where heather and boulders, remnants of the glaciers from the last ice age, dot the landscape. Two streams converge at a rock adorned with Neolithic cup symbols. Close by, there's another cave believed to be home to fairies. Historically, fairies in Scotland were far less friendly than J. M. Barrie's Tinker Bell or the "Disneyfied" fairies depicted in movies and on TV today. These caves would have been keenly avoided by the ancient peoples who lived there, fearing being trapped in the fairy kingdom for eternity.

Along with its ancient Celtic connections, some believe Schiehallion to be the sacred sanctuary of the Knights Templar, known as Mount Heredom. According to an esoteric tradition, there was a primary trinity of holy mountains, Mount Moriah in Palestine, Mount Sinai in Egypt and Mount Heredom, a mythological mountain in the far north where the gods held their assembly. There is also a legend that three Templar knights sought refuge in its caverns, perpetuating the mystery surrounding the mountain's hidden depths.

Throughout history, tales of a goddess known as Cailleach Bheur haunting Schiehallion have captured imaginations. Revered as a hag goddess of winter, she is believed to be reborn on Samhain (Halloween) and to linger until Beltane. Legend holds that at Beltane, a festival marking the beginning of the pagan summer, she undergoes a transformation, either into a standing stone or a maiden, leaving her mark on the mountain with the Sgrìob na Caillich (the scratching of the old woman), known now as Cailleach's Furrow. Cailleach's Furrow refers to a geological feature attributed to the Cailleach, believed to have been formed by her ploughing the land during the winter months. Additionally, a fairy well on the mountain is sometimes associated with her, where young girls make offerings of flowers on Beltane or May Day.

In addition to its mystical significance, Schiehallion gained fame as the location of one of the first large-scale contour maps drawn in the eighteenth century. This mapping project, known as the Schiehallion Experiment, led by astronomer Royal Nevil Maskelyne and his team, aimed to measure the Earth's mass and density by studying the gravitational pull of the mountain. This groundbreaking experiment marked a significant milestone in the history of science and cartography. The stories surrounding Schiehallion reflect its dual significance as both a mystical landmark in Gaelic folklore and a site of scientific importance in the history of astronomy.

The Perthshire region, including Kinloch Rannoch, offers a perfect blend of history, scenery, and outdoor exploration, making it an ideal destination for those seeking to experience the best of Scotland's countryside. If you've ever visited, you'll understand why my parents were so keen to move there.

They bought a huge, old, and run-down property that was perfect for them: Liarn Farm on the north shore of Loch Rannoch, complete with over two hundred acres of land. Part of this expansive property included the historic drovers' road known as the "Road to the Isles", which passed through the estate. Exploring further, they discovered the remnants of old stables, the ruins of ancient blackhouses, and a collection of ghost stories passed down by the previous owner, a woman who had lived there her whole life, since the late nineteenth century.

The Ghost Light

The first story might be more accurately described as a UFO or "spirit light" tale in modern terms. It doesn't involve apparitions, noises, or everyday objects moving, but rather a glowing light observed moving across the surface of Loch Rannoch. It always appears at night, consistently emanating from the same location, then travels down across the Black Wood on the south shore of Loch Rannoch and then invariably disappears at the same spot.

In 1937, author Alistair MacGregor wrote in his book *The Peat-fire Flame* that "a light in the form of a ball sometimes is seen skimming the surface of the water. This light always rises at the same point, travels the same short distance, and likewise disappears at the same place".

The farmhouse on Liarn overlooked the shores of Loch Rannoch, offering an incredible view along its fifteen-mile length. On a particularly dark evening (I've never experienced such darkness until my first night at Liarn. It's pitch black and deathly quiet), my mum prepared for bed. She climbed the stairs and glanced out the landing window, which overlooked the loch.

To her surprise, she could see a light out on the loch – not above the loch but emanating from under the waves, illuminating the water around it. Confused, she watched this light for a few seconds until it gradually dimmed and faded out of sight.

Given the Ghost Light is supposed to be seen above and skimming the water and not below the waves, she figured that what she had seen was a fisherman lowering a light into the loch and not the fabled Ghost Light of Rannoch.

The Carriage

Our second story takes place on the lands of Liarn itself. Due to its location, above the banks of the loch, to reach the farmhouse you'd have to travel the old road leading up to the farm buildings, which is now used as a driveway.

No longer than a quarter mile, there are, as yet, no electric lights to guide you up the drive to the farm, so you can understand how unnerving an experience it would be to walk this route in the dead of night, something I only had the courage to do once. Now, imagine you are walking this in the pitch black, and in the distance you hear the rumble of wheels over gravel, then the unmistakable pounding of horses' hooves and the sounds of braying growing quickly ever closer. For centuries, the thundering approach of a spectral black carriage has echoed up the drive to Liarn Farm, climaxing with the eerie sight of the carriage, drawn by two ghostly horses, halting outside the farmhouse door.

I don't know much about the origins of this story, but if memory serves, the carriage – like the Ban Sith (banshee) – is meant to be a portent of death and disaster. It's said that misfortune or death follows witnesses shortly after sighting it. Although I've only walked the driveway at night once, I've stood at the door on many occasions after dark, listening for the distant whinny of horses. Thankfully, I never encountered this horrifying spectre.

The Ghost Stone

Our third and final story is my favourite of the three. The road to Liarn is a long, mainly single track that meanders along the shoreline of the loch. It's a delightful route to drive; in fact, not too long ago, it was used for rally car racing; and some early PlayStation games even featured this demanding route as a driving challenge. There is a bit of a landmark, for want of a better expression, that signals you've entered onto Liarn Farm land – a simple stone on the north side of the road. The stone isn't massive, nor a mythical standing stone, but it's an important stone nonetheless, and this is where our ghost emanates from, literally.

Before motor cars, horses served as our primary mode of transport. The local postman would set off on his rounds on horseback, starting from Kinloch Rannoch at the eastern end of the loch. He would travel anti-clockwise around the shores, delivering mail to various locations, before eventually returning to Kinloch Rannoch. This round trip must have been quite a lengthy and laborious journey for him.

On one occasion, as he approached the boundary of Liarn, he neared what would become known as the "Ghost Stone".

His horse let out a loud whinny and stopped abruptly, nearly throwing the equally terrified postman from its back. Just then, a white mist emerged from the stone, gradually forming into the shape of a blurry white figure standing in the middle of the road. Although he could see this spirit, he couldn't discern any features or clothing; it was simply a white figure resembling a person. Spooked and frightened, his horse turned and bolted, with the terrified postman clinging on to the reins desperately.

It's said that after this, the postman's horse would never go past that spot no matter how much he tried. This meant our poor postman couldn't go past Liarn Farm and had to instead make his way to its nearest neighbour, then double back and go round the loch the other way.

Having had the opportunity to spend considerable time in the stunning landscapes of Rannoch and Perthshire, I cherish the memories of family holidays that still fill me with nostalgia and awe. The majestic Munros, peaceful glens, and meandering rivers have always held a special place in my heart, along with the rich historical heritage embodied by Perth.

My mother's deep affection for the area greatly influenced me as her dream of living amidst the scenic beauty of Kinloch Rannoch became a reality. Together with my father, they embarked on a new adventure, immersing themselves in the natural splendour of Rannoch Moor and the imposing presence of Schiehallion.

Stories like those from Liarn Farm are why I've written this book. They risk fading away and deserve a place in our collective memory. Other than the source mentioned previously, I can find no other record of these accounts.

Recounting these tales reminds us to preserve our cultural heritage and pass down stories through generations. They're more than just entertainment; they connect us to our past and the land.

By documenting unreported ghostly encounters, like those at Liarn Farm, I aim to prevent these stories from being forgotten. They're part of Scotland's history, offering insights into past beliefs and fears, tied to local landscapes and landmarks.

While it's possible that the origins of these legends are connected to illegal activities in the area, such as illicit stills (secret whisky production), which served as warnings to deter people from certain places, I prefer to consider the content of the stories with some credibility. These elements add depth to the narratives, reflecting the complexities of the past.

As our world changes, these stories can easily vanish. But preserving them is crucial for understanding our shared heritage and the mysteries of the past.

Including Liarn Farm's story in this book keeps these legends alive, captivating readers for generations. They're not just ghost stories; they're woven into Scotland's cultural fabric, inviting exploration of its rich history.

CHAPTER 18
SLIGACHAN, THE ISLE OF SKYE

The Isle of Skye, with its rugged landscapes and breathtaking beauty, epitomises the wild allure of Scotland. The landscape is characterised by its breathtaking beauty and dramatic contrasts. From the rugged peaks of the Cuillin mountains to the sweeping expanses of moorland and coastline, Skye offers a diverse tapestry of natural wonders.

At the heart of the island lie the jagged Cuillins, their serrated ridges towering above the landscape, shrouded in mist and myth. These majestic peaks, with names like Sgurr nan Gillean and Bruach na Frithe, provide a playground for mountaineers and a sense of awe for all who behold them.

Away from the mountains, Skye's landscape unfolds in a series of dramatic vistas and hidden gems. Deep glens cut through the terrain, their sides clothed in ancient woodlands and cascading waterfalls. Lochs dot the landscape, their still waters reflecting the ever-changing skies above. The coastline of Skye is equally enchanting, with rugged cliffs, hidden coves, and sweeping beaches where echoes of the island's prehistoric past can still be found in the ancient rock formations and geological wonders scattered along the shore. Sea stacks rise defiantly from the waves, while sea eagles soar overhead, their cries echoing across the wide expanse of the sea. Throughout the island, remnants of its geological history are visible in the form of volcanic rock formations, basalt columns, and sea cliffs sculpted by millennia of erosion. Skye was once part of a supervolcano that stretched to Glencoe, leaving behind a landscape shaped by ancient forces. Yet amidst this raw beauty, there is a sense of tranquillity and timelessness that pervades the landscape, inviting visitors to lose themselves in its grandeur and mystery.

Skye's natural wonders can only be rivalled by its rich history, a history that stretches back thousands of years. From ancient times, Skye has been inhabited by various peoples, each leaving their mark on the land. For centuries preceding the formation of the Scottish nation, Skye and the surrounding islands were under the rule of the Lord of the Isles. The Lordship of the Isles, a feudal title of Scottish nobility, held sway over the Hebrides and parts of the western mainland of Scotland. Skye, being one of the largest and strategically vital islands in the Hebrides, served as a significant stronghold for the Lords of the Isles.

Throughout the mediaeval period, Skye served as a power base for the MacLeod and MacDonald clans, who were among the most prominent families to hold the title of Lord of the Isles. These clans ruled over Skye and the surrounding islands, exerting considerable influence over trade, politics, and warfare in the region. The Lords of the Isles often clashed with the Scottish crown and other rival factions for control of Skye and its valuable resources. Skirmishes and battles were common as various clans vied for dominance over the island and its lucrative trade routes. The castle strongholds of Dunvegan and Dunscaith were particularly important centres of power for the Lords of the Isles on Skye. These formidable fortresses served as symbols of authority and provided strategic positions from which to defend the island against external threats.

Despite periods of instability and conflict, the Lordship of the Isles endured for centuries, shaping the history and culture of Skye and the wider Hebridean region. Even today, the legacy of the Lords of the Isles is evident in the castles, clan heritage, and folklore that continue to define the island's identity. The island's history is intertwined with the clans that called it home, none more prominent than the Macleods and the MacDonalds. The Macleods, known for their stronghold at Dunvegan Castle, held sway over much of Skye for centuries, their influence felt in the land they governed and the stories they left behind. Their rivalry with the MacDonalds, another powerful clan with roots deeply embedded in the island's soil, often sparked conflict and shaped the course of Skye's history. Amidst the clan feuds and battles for dominance, Skye became a melting pot of cultures and traditions, with Norse, Gaelic, and Celtic influences leaving their indelible imprint on the island's identity.

Today, echoes of Skye's storied past can still be heard in the ancient ruins, standing stones, and brochs scattered across the landscape. Each tells a tale of the people who once called this land home, adding another layer of intrigue to Skye's already captivating allure. One of the most brutal conflicts between the MacDonalds and Macleods occurred in 1398 in a remote location known as Harta Corrie, near Glen Sligachan. Harta Corrie is surrounded by imposing peaks and is hidden away, off the beaten track within a rugged and remote landscape.

The chief of the MacDonald clan had fervently asserted his claim to the title of Lord of the Isles years earlier, igniting numerous bloody conflicts with rival clans. As his forces swelled in strength and resolve, they launched a daring invasion of Skye to substantiate their claims. The occupying Macleods, longstanding adversaries of the MacDonalds, vehemently refused to acknowledge their claim, setting the stage for a fierce struggle for dominance.

As morning broke and the sun cast its golden light upon the rocks of the corrie, tension hung thick in the air. The MacDonalds and Macleods prepared for a brutal battle for supremacy. The first cry rang out, echoing across the rugged terrain as the two clans clashed in a savage melee. Wave after wave of Highlanders charged at each other with fierce determination, swords flashing in the early light as they engaged in a deadly dance of combat. The air resounded with the clash of steel and the cries of the wounded, mingling with the primal roars of warriors locked in mortal combat. From dawn till dusk, the battle raged on unabated, neither side yielding an inch of ground. In the end, it was the MacDonalds who emerged victorious, their foes vanquished.

Contemporary accounts suggest that not a single Macleod survived, not one. Legend has it that the bodies of the fallen were piled around a massive rock, with a rowan tree growing from its summit, giving rise to the grim moniker "the Bloody Stone". For years after, locals shunned the dark depths of Harta Corrie, avoiding it after dark. They attributed the haunting moans and whispers heard in the night to the restless spirits of the fallen Highlanders.

The Phantom Highlanders

However, with the growing popularity of hillwalking in the late twentieth century, more and more people began to visit the corrie, defying its haunted reputation. Amidst the tales of spooky whispers and haunting moans, one story stands out – that of two geology students from Oxford, who dared to camp in Harta Corrie during the 1960s. One of the men, Sir Patrick Skipwith, would go on to document what they witnessed that evening.

The day had been uneventful; the men had explored the glen and the corrie, taking samples and enjoying the remoteness of their surroundings. As dusk beckoned, they made camp by one of the many rivers running through the area. After a hearty meal, it was time for both men to retire to their tents for the night.

The sky was clear, and the moon was bright, illuminating the corrie around them with an otherworldly light. Sir Patrick, an experienced outdoorsman and normally a sound sleeper, found himself stirring from his slumber. Unsure why he had woken, he sat up in his sleeping bag, rubbed his eyes, and listened intently for any sound that could explain why he'd been disturbed. The only sound he could hear was the gentle snoring of his companion coming from their tent, permeating an otherwise silent night.

Curious, he quietly unzipped his tent and peered out into the inky darkness, looking to his left and right before fixing his gaze directly in front of him. As his eyes adjusted, for a moment, he thought he caught movement on the side of the hill opposite his tent. Assuming what he was seeing was a stag, they number plenty in the glens of Skye, he watched it for a while, waiting for the proof that his hunch was correct. After a few seconds, he noticed more movement to the right of the initial figure. Now intrigued and convinced it was a trick of the light, he decided he wanted a closer look so gingerly took a step outside his tent.

With his improved vantage point, he was now able to clearly see, not one, not two but dozens of what he described as Highlanders scrambling across the rocks on the hill opposite, only fifty or so yards away from his tent. His mind was racing; why were these men dressed like this? Why were they moving without the aid of modern camping lights, and why was there no sound coming from them?

After what felt like an eternity, he shook himself to his senses and woke his walking partner. On hearing Sir Patrick's breathlessly rushed story, he naturally assumed he was dreaming or had maybe indulged in a wee whisky when he'd retired for the night. But after some vigorous encouragement, bordering on being dragged out of his tent, he too could see the phantom Highlanders making their slow deliberate traverse along the mountainside. Astonished, the men watched for what they estimated to be ten minutes as the ghostly visitors silently made their way over the hill before mysteriously fading out of sight and disappearing.

Sir Patrick also visited the area some three years later, with a larger group of travelling companions, and they again witnessed the ghostly clansmen making their way across the mountainside before disappearing into the night. Had the campers witnessed the spectral echoes of the events leading up to the battle of Harta Corrie?

Not all hauntings near Sligachan are ancient or remote like our phantom Highlanders; there's another, more modern tale waiting to be told – a haunting with origins closer to our time.

The Ghost Car

In recent years, reports have circulated of a mysterious phantom car that roams the lonely roads near Sligachan, its headlights piercing the darkness of the night; the car is most often witnessed on the old coast road that goes from Sligachan past "the Braes" to Portree, the capital of Skye. The car in question? A 1934 Austin, its vintage frame gleaming in the moonlight as it glides silently along the winding roads. Witnesses speak of encountering the spectral vehicle when the moon is high and the mist hangs low, its form appearing suddenly before vanishing into the night like a wisp of smoke. Some claim to have heard the distant sound of an engine revving, though the car leaves no trace of tire marks or exhaust fumes behind. It's a modern mystery that adds yet another layer to the enigmatic allure of Sligachan's haunting landscape.

The first recorded sighting happened in 1941 and is documented in Peter Underwood's *Gazetteer of Scottish and Irish Ghosts* and tells of when Dr Allan McDonald saw the car as he drove along the dark and windy road home. "I was motoring along the road," he explained, "when I noticed a car travelling very quickly towards me over the hill. Its speed really was terrific and I drew into the side of the road to let [it] pass, but it never came abreast of me. I waited a while, then proceeded forward and found that the car had completely vanished. There was simply nowhere for it to have gone."

A few years later, Donald Mckinnon from Sconsa also witnessed the car speeding along the road before vanishing right in front of his eyes. Strangely, his son also saw the car moving at a supernatural speed before also completely vanishing in front of him.

The local postman, Neil McDairmid, saw the car early one winter morning. He said, "I had been out with the mail to Sligachan. There had been a full moon, but it had gone down. As I drove along, a cold chill suddenly swept over me. I looked down to the shore side and saw an old Austin travelling very fast, with one light burning bright at the front and a kind of dim glow inside the car. I could plainly see that there was no one at the wheel. It tore ahead of me and veered to the right, then simply disappeared."

From what I've been able to ascertain, there are a couple of stories that could explain the origins of the ghostly automobile. One version tells of a farmhand who met an untimely death many years ago when his car smashed into a stone wall on the bridge at Sligachan. Another involves a truly tragic event where a clergyman had a terrible accident while trying to drive onto the ferry to the mainland. His accelerator pedal seemed to stick, causing his car to burst through the ferry doors at the other end and plunge into the water. Sadly, he was not alone in the car: at least two women and a young child were with him, and none survived.

There is also a report of a policeman who was driving the Sligachan road late one night and stopped to aid what he thought was an injured victim of a serious road accident, standing by the side of the road. When he got out of his police car to investigate, he could find no one where he'd originally seen the figure, and there was no sign of a car crash. Within a week, however, he was called back to the same spot to attend a fatal car accident. Is it possible that the vision he saw was a glimpse of the future?

Strangely, I have a good friend who is originally from Skye but who now lives in Edinburgh. He swears that he and his wife saw a young girl standing at the side of the road where the ghost car is regularly sighted. She was wearing what they described as a tattered old hessian dress. She looked at them as they passed, but when they looked back, she was no longer there, and there was nowhere she could have gone. What is it about Sligachan and this stretch of road that causes so much spectral activity?

I included these tales in my book to highlight an often-overlooked aspect of the Isle of Skye. The island is famous for its natural attractions, like the Quiraing and the Cuillin mountain range, as well as its mystical legends surrounding the Fairy Pools and the Fairy Glen. However, the stories of hauntings are less known, and by sharing these ghostly legends, I aim to provide a fuller picture of Skye's rich and varied history. By sharing these accounts, I aim to deepen readers' understanding of Skye's rich folklore and history.

These haunting tales, embedded in the island's culture, offer a unique perspective on its mystical charm, making Skye not only a place of endless history and natural beauty but also a land of enduring mystery and intrigue.

CHAPTER 19
LITTLEDEAN TOWER

As you may have noticed, the "Rough Wooing" was a pivotal and impactful moment in Scottish and English history, and this next story also finds its roots in that moment. The period was characterised by a series of military campaigns and political manoeuvres aimed at securing the marriage between the two-year-old Mary, Queen of Scots, and the six-year-old son of Henry VIII of England, Edward VI.

The term "rough" in the name refers to the aggressive and forceful tactics employed by the English forces under Henry VIII and later his son, Edward VI, to coerce Scotland into agreeing to the marriage alliance. The conflict involved English incursions into Scottish territory, raids, sieges, and battles, resulting in widespread destruction and suffering for the Scottish population. Invading English forces, under commanders such as the Earl of Hertford, strategically targeted Scottish towns, castles, and religious institutions to weaken Scotland's resistance and compel compliance with English demands.

The conflict saw several large-scale battles, notably the Battle of Ancrum Moor in 1545, the Battle of Pinkie Cleugh in 1547, and the siege of Haddington from 1548 to 1549.

After English troops routed the numerically superior Scottish army at the battle of Pinkie Cleugh, where an army of Scots numbering up to twenty-two thousand men were defeated by an English army of less than seventeen thousand, James Hamilton, the Regent of Scotland, lay siege to the strategically important Burgh of Haddington. From July 1548 to September 1549, Scottish forces besieged the well-entrenched English army occupying the small market town. Positioned near the border with England, it served as a key stronghold for controlling access to both Edinburgh and the eastern coastal regions. Control Haddington and you control a vital transportation route.

Fifteen thousand English soldiers, bolstered by around two hundred Albanian troops, dug in and fortified the town, hoping that the far smaller Scottish army would run out of supplies long before they did, or use up their dwindling resources attacking the formidable defences. The English troops were battle-hardened campaigners, and they put that experience to good use, turning Haddington into a fortress that by all accounts rivalled the famously impregnable Turin.

For over a year, the Scots bombarded the town, bringing in cannon from all over the country to test the English defences, even the great Scottish gun "thrawinmouth" was brought from Dunbar Castle to help with the siege, and French troops brought additional guns to help break the English barricades.

Although the siege ultimately ended due to constant harrying by the Scots, with night-time raids common, sickness spreading through the English ranks, and changing political circumstances, there were some notable skirmishes in the fourteen-month-long siege. One such story became known as "Tuesday's Chase".

Nestled along the River Tweed, approximately three miles from the historic village of St Boswells, lie the remnants of Littledean Tower. This once imposing structure, traditionally the stronghold of the Kers of Littledean, commands a strategic position on the riverbanks, offering sweeping views of the surrounding landscape, crucial for monitoring approaching threats and controlling the movement along the river. Once a formidable four-storey oblong tower, its imposing stature bore witness to centuries of history. Constructed upon the remnants of a former fortress, legend has it that stones from the ancient castle were repurposed in the construction of this more modern stronghold.

In 1544, amid the violent raids of the eight-year war, the castle suffered devastation as English troops launched a relentless assault, leaving it badly battered and in ruins. To fortify its defences, a massive D-shaped tower was erected. This newly constructed tower boasted sturdy rubble walls measuring 1.8 metres in thickness, faced with finely cut ashlar. Rising four stories tall with an additional garret (a room or unfinished part of a house just under the roof), the tower not only reinforced Littledean's fortifications but also provided ample additional living space.

Littledean remained in use until the late eighteenth century. With the peace brought by the Act of Union, it is said the Kers opted to relocate to nearby Nenthorn House. Did they relocate to a more modern house, or did they relocate, as many believe, to escape the events that occurred behind the ancient fortress's thick stone walls?

The following story was published in *Notes on the Folk-lore of the Northern Counties of England and the Borders* by William Henderson (1879).

"The ancient tower of Littledean, on the Tweedside, had long been haunted by the spirit of an old lady, once its mistress, who had been a covetous, grasping woman, and oppressive to the poor. Tradition averred that she had amassed a large sum of money by thrift or extortion, and now could not rest in her grave because of it.

"Still, in spite of its ghost, Littledean Tower was inhabited by a laird and his family, who found no fault with their place of abode, and were not much troubled by thoughts of the supernatural world.

"One Saturday evening, however, a servant-girl, who was cleaning shoes in the kitchen by herself, suddenly observed an elf-light shining on the floor. While she gazed on it, it disappeared, and in its place stood an old woman wrapped in a brown cloak, who muttered something about being cold, and asked to warm herself at the fire.

"The girl readily consented, and seeing that her visitor's shoes were wet, and her toes peeping out blue and cold from their tips, she good-naturedly offered to dry and clean the shoes, and did so.

"The old lady, touched by this attention, confessed herself frankly to be the apparition that haunted the house. 'My gold wud na let me rest,' said she, 'but I'll tell ye where it lies; 'tis 'neath the lowest step o' the Tower stairs. Take the laird there an' tell him what I now tell ye; then dig up the treasure, and put it in his hands. An' tell him to part it in two shares: one share let him keep, for he's master here now; the other share he maun part again, and gie half to you, for ye are a kind lassie and true, and half he maun gie to the poor o' Maxton,

> the old folk and the fatherless bairns, and them that need it most. Do this and I sail rest in my grave, where I've no rested yet, and never will I trouble the house mair till the day o' doom.' The girl rubbed her eyes, looked again, and behold the old woman was gone!
>
> "Next morning the young servant took her master to the spot which had been indicated to her, and told him what had taken place. The stone was removed, and the treasure discovered, and divided according to the instructions given. The laird, being blessed with a goodly family of sturdy lads and smiling maidens, found no difficulty in disposing of his share. The servant-girl, so richly endowed, found a good husband ere the year had passed. The poor of Maxton for the first time in their lives blessed the old lady of Littledean, and never was the ancient tower troubled again by ghost or apparition."

Legend has it that in the 1600s, a former laird of the tower had a reputation as a tyrannical figure, known for his violent temper, love of drink, and for the cruel treatment of his family and servants. There is a story that, unhappy with how a stable boy had saddled his horse, he had the boy trampled to death under the hooves of the very horse he'd been tasked with saddling.

His reputation for brutality drew like-minded men to the castle, where they gathered for late-night feasts and revelry. Margaret, his long-suffering wife, often bore the brunt of his anger. She dreaded his drinking sessions and did her best to avoid drawing his attention during those times. That wasn't always possible.

On one occasion, during such a gathering, the laird demanded his wife's presence. When she refused, he forcibly dragged her into the festivities, holding her forcefully against the wall so she could not escape; he then began subjecting her to brutal abuse, all in front of his visitors, before casting her to the cold, castle floor.

Eventually, the laird released her and let her go, but as she hurried away, he shouted one last insult, declaring he would sooner wed a fiend from Hell, for such a wife would have more warmth than the woman he married. Margaret could stand the abuse no longer and snapped back, "You will live to regret these words!"

The laird persisted in drinking until heavily intoxicated and long after his guests had left Littledean. Fuelled by copious amounts of alcohol and adrenaline coursing through his veins, he saddled up his horse and, heedless of his staff's warnings, rode off into the night, into a once-in-a-century thunderstorm.

Ignoring the weather at first, he rode on, but as the severity of the storm became apparent, he desperately sought refuge. By a stroke of luck, he chanced upon a secluded cottage nestled amidst the darkness.

The door to the cottage was open, and a warm light emanated from the doorway, illuminating the darkness around it. Dismounting his horse, he cautiously approached, unsure what to expect, as, knowing his land like he did, he had no memory of a cottage like this on his property.

The closer he got, the more the storm seemed to abate, and quietness settled around. He was soon able to see through the rain-lashed window and, for a second, thought he saw dark shapes moving around the corners of the cottage but put it down to a trick of the light.

Peering through the door, he encountered a woman of captivating beauty sitting peacefully by a spinning wheel. He attempted to communicate with her, but instead of speaking to him, she turned, looked at him and, with a maniacal laugh, snapped the thread she was holding in two. At this, he took fright, quickly mounted his horse and galloped away.

Time passed, and the laird grew to become obsessed with the mysterious woman; he searched in vain for the cottage, night after night, but without success. Close to giving up, he ventured out one last time only to encounter her again by chance near the tower. The beautiful woman was standing by a river in a clearing. When she saw him, she held out her arms, smiled and beckoned him to her. Then she guided him to some trees near the tower and said that she would always meet him there.

Despite being in sight of his marital home, the laird ventured out night after night to indulge his passions with this mysterious woman. Although he attempted to keep their affair secret, Lady Margaret discovered the truth and confronted him, throwing her wedding ring in his face. She vowed to leave him, and on hearing this, he simply turned and walked away.

Her curiosity got the better of her, and she paid two of the male servants to venture into the woods to where the adulterous lovers would meet, in the hope she could uncover the identity of her husband's obsession, but when they arrived at their meeting place, they found it empty. Deciding to wait, their patience soon paid off, and they saw the laird's lover wandering through the trees. As she drew closer, the men revealed themselves, and the startled mysterious woman ran off into the trees, with both men giving chase. Closing in, the men were sure they came upon the woman behind a large oak tree, but when they rounded it, they found only a large hare that hopped past the surprised servants.

Returning that evening to Littledean, the men found Lady Margaret beside herself with worry, as the laird was missing. Deciding it was too late to mount a meaningful search for the missing man, they agreed to wait until first light to put together their search party.

However, during the night, the laird's horse was seen galloping through the trees, heading towards the tower, carrying the unconscious laird on its back. The horse arrived at Littledean, sweating and snorting heavily, as if it was terrified and had been running for its life.

The unconscious laird soon came to, but when he did, he was ashen-faced and shaking with grim fright. Pressed on what had happened to him and why he had returned so late in such a state, he told those gathered that while he was riding home, he noticed a hare running alongside his horse. This hare was soon joined by several others, who, no matter how fast he galloped, managed to keep pace with the laird. The hares had a supernatural speed and way to them; they would run in and out of the horse's legs, often jumping up to saddle height towards the now panicked laird. Eventually the laird drew his sword, swinging wildly while unsuccessfully attempting to trample them under his horse's hooves. Again and again he swung, but each time missed until, with one mighty swing, his blade connected with the paw of one hare, severing it clean off, and with this, the huske of hares vanished into the undergrowth.

This would not signal the end of the encounter, for instead of falling to the ground, the paw somehow made its way into the laird's pistol holster. The laird continued his long ride, but found himself miles from where he thought he should be, so spurred his horse on to ride for Littledean. When he finished his story, he reached into his holster to show those gathered the paw he'd severed. Instead of feeling the soft fur of the paw, his hand was instead grabbed by something far more familiar, and he threw it down on the ground in front of him. "It grabbed me!" he yelled. And as the crowd gathered looked to see what the wicked laird had thrown on the ground, they were horrified to see the severed hand of a young woman. Impaling the hand on the end of his sword, he took it to the river to rid himself of this unearthly trophy in the dark waters below.

As he stood, he realised he was not alone, and turning to his left, he caught sight of his lover sitting on a stone by the side of the river. "You took my hand from me; now it will be with you forever," she rasped. To his horror, he could no longer see the beautiful young woman he'd grown besotted with; instead he was confronted by the leering face of a haggard old woman holding her arm up in defiance at him.

The laird fled back to the safety of Littledean and took to his bedroom to rest. Collapsing in a chair by the fire in his bedroom, he placed his hand in his pocket to retrieve his tobacco, but instead pulled out the severed hand he'd thrown in the river earlier. Throwing this out the window, he retired to his bed to sleep and, on placing his hand under his pillow…found another severed hand.

As morning broke, Lady Margaret's servant ascended to the laird's chamber to summon him for breakfast. Opening the locked door, she was met with the chilling sight of him lying lifeless in the centre of the room, his face twisted in terror, his neck bearing distinct marks of fingers, a haunting testimony to his final moments.

After the laird's death, rumours spread through the countryside about the eerie events that took place within Littledean Tower. Stories of a tyrant undone by his own actions mingled with legends of ghosts and vengeful spirits haunting the fortress. The laird's tragic fate was a stark reminder of the consequences of cruelty and folly. Lady Margaret, left to bear her husband's legacy, found some comfort in knowing that justice, though delayed, had been served in its own mysterious way.

As the sun rose over the Scottish Borders, casting shadows on the rugged landscape, Littledean Tower stood as a silent witness to the enduring mysteries within its ancient stones, a testament to the turbulent history and ghostly whispers of the past. Thus, the legend of Littledean Tower endured, a cautionary tale woven into the land, where truth and folklore intertwined, shrouded in the mists of time.

I included Littledean Tower in this book because, despite its current state as a forgotten shell, it holds significant historical value. Its walls have witnessed tales of power, downfall, and supernatural events that deserve to be remembered. The story of Littledean Tower is not just about a haunted castle; it's a classic narrative about the consequences of moral choices and the enduring impact of history. By revisiting Littledean Tower, I aim to bring its rich past to light, reminding readers of the lessons it holds and ensuring that its legacy is not lost to time.

CHAPTER 20
BROOMHILL HOUSE, LARKHALL

Before the discovery of coal, Larkhall was a rural area characterised by its isolation and small villages, such as Millheugh. The economy was primarily agricultural, and the community was relatively cut off from the rest of the country. Life revolved around traditional rural activities, and there was limited economic development or population growth.

However, with the discovery of coal, Larkhall underwent a significant transformation. The mining industry boomed, bringing an influx of workers and rapid urbanisation to the area. The once predominantly rural landscape became dotted with collieries and mining settlements. The economy shifted from agriculture to industrial-scale mining, which in turn provided employment opportunities, attracting people from various parts of the country. This quickly led to a substantial increase in population and brought about considerable changes in the social and economic fabric of Larkhall and its surrounding areas, almost overnight.

East of Larkhall, the terrain slopes down towards the River Clyde, while to the west, it descends towards the River Avon.

Just beyond the ancient village of Millheugh, which has roots extending all the way back to the Dark Ages, lies the renowned beauty spot of Morgan Glen. Overlooking this glen on the slopes, until recently, stood the imposing Broomhill House.

The scant remains of Broomhill House now serve as a sad reminder of centuries of history and heritage, its presence once looming large over the surrounding landscape. In 1568, when the building was called the Castle of Auld Machan, it's said that the house was attacked and burnt to the ground by Sir William Drury, governor of Berwick. Afterwards, the building was repaired, and a turnpike (spiral) staircase added.

In 1792, the building was described as "Buildings. – Dalsers house, the residence of Captain James Hamilton of Broomhill, is a neat modern building, standing upon an eminence, near the village of Dalferf, and commands a charming prospect, both up and down the Clyde. Broomhill house, which also belongs to the fame gentleman, and which was the feat of the ancient family of the Hamiltons of Broomhill, (the elder branch of which were created Lords Belhaven), stands upon the top of the banks of the river Avon, in a fine airy situation, having a most agreeable view of the country around, and of the river Avon, with its pleasant banks. Mr Hamilton, induced by the remarkable beauty of the situation, is now building another house, upon an eminence above the village of Dalferf; which commands one of the most extensive and delightful prospects that can well be imagined."

Due to its position on the slopes above Morgan Glen, Broomhill enjoyed a commanding view of the scenic landscape that once surrounded it. The house itself later suffered severe damage from a fire in 1943, marking another tragic chapter in its long history. Despite efforts to preserve and restore it, the fire left the once-stately mansion in ruins, forever altering its appearance and significance.

Surrounded by sprawling grounds and lush gardens, Broomhill once provided the Hamiltons with a peaceful retreat, offering them sanctuary from the busy world beyond its gates.

The Hamiltons held a significant presence in the area for generations, their influence deeply rooted in the local landscape, community and industry. Known for their military prowess and political alliances, they played crucial roles in shaping Scotland's destiny. Over time, they acquired vast estates, including Broomhill House in Larkhall, showcasing their wealth and influence.

Throughout the nineteenth century, the McNeil-Hamiltons lived in Broomhill, managing extensive land holdings and village properties. Their influence went beyond land ownership, as they held significant power within the community, exemplified by Captain Henry Montgomery McNeil-Hamilton.

Captain McNeil-Hamilton, born in 1872, inherited the estate at a tender age following his father's passing in 1883. His upbringing was steeped in military tradition, and he pursued a career in the military, eventually rising to the rank of captain in the Cameronians. Despite his prestigious lineage and military achievements, his personal life was marred by marital discord; rumours of affairs plagued the couple and eventually led to a separation from his wife, Edith Gertrude Thomson Carmichael, in 1910.

Before divorcing, Captain McNeil-Hamilton and his wife had four children – one son and three daughters. However, their marriage was fraught with unhappiness. While serving in South Africa during the second Boer war, he met and would become romantically involved with Sita, the woman who would go on to be known as the Lady of Larkhall. As the captain was already in an unhappy marriage, Sita was brought to Broomhall as his mistress, though under the guise of a servant. There's no doubt this led to the separation of the captain and Edith in 1910, and despite his personal issues, McNeil-Hamilton continued to live in Broomhill until his passing in 1924.

Due to the racial prejudices of the time, Sita's life was not a happy one, and she rarely ventured beyond the house's boundaries. She was often seen walking alone in the woods surrounding Broomhall, looking unhappy. Then one day, she disappeared.

A local resident, Mrs Perry, remembered seeing Sita at 10pm one night, following her evening meal. The next day, Sita was nowhere to be found. Asking around, Mrs Perry was told that Sita had been unhappy with life in Larkhall and had left to return home to India. This seemed strange to Mrs Perry, as the last train from Larkhall was at 9pm, an hour before she'd seen her, and no one had seen Sita walk the considerable distance to the train station.

Since then, Broomhill House has become entwined with the Lady of Larkhall legend, with sightings and stories firmly embedded in the area's folklore, and for one local resident, the legend may well have become a reality.

For privacy reasons, I've changed the names, but for Katriona MacDonald, there was an added familial link to this enduring tale. Katriona often pondered why her grandmother Morag Turnbull remained so attached to Broomhill House, continuing to visit it even at the age of eighty-two in 1939. Morag began working at Broomhill at the age of twelve and stayed until the onset of the Second World War, rising from maid to housekeeper.

During the 1920s and '30s, when the McNeil-Hamilton family wasn't residing there, the house was primarily under the care of caretakers, affording Morag the liberty to come and go. The house temporarily served as army accommodation during the war and suffered significant damage from a fire in 1943. In 1954, the family sold the remaining land and property to Mrs Euphemia Hamilton.

Morag was known for her stories about the Lady of Larkhall, which she passed on to her son and, in turn, to her granddaughter, Katriona. As a result, Katriona, like many Larkhall residents, grew up hearing about the Lady. However, her connection to the legend would become far more personal than she had anticipated. While in her late thirties, Katriona started having a recurring dream. Initially, she didn't associate it with the Lady of Larkhall despite being familiar with the stories.

The dream, which started as vague and unclear, became more vivid over time. In it, she found herself – or someone who looked like an older version of her – in a room with an ornate fireplace, a clock, and a candlestick. The room had green curtains, a piano, and a firescreen with a red rose. To her left stood a tall, striking Asian woman, and to her right was a man with an aristocratic look and piercing eyes. The dream then showed a man's hand, wearing a gold ring with a black stone, lifting a candlestick and striking the woman on the head. The woman fell, and her body was dragged through the house, across a black-and-white marble floor, and down a staircase into a cellar. Despite the presence of blood, the body remained just inside the door.

Katriona experienced more dreams that seemed to occur in different parts of the same house. One depicted a nursery with a young, deformed boy and a broken rocking horse, where the woman tried to comfort the child. Another dream showed hooded figures performing a ritual in a cellar or vault. Troubled by the vividness of these dreams, Katriona couldn't help but wonder if the woman might be connected to the legend of the Lady of Larkhall.

Morag, a practical woman, was not prone to inventing stories, especially in an area rich with folklore. She claimed not only to have seen the ghost of the Lady but to have interacted with the woman herself during her time at Broomhill. Given her grandmother's credibility, Katriona felt compelled to investigate. According to Morag, the Lady was from India and lived at Broomhill for about two years around the turn of the century. One evening, she left unexpectedly, supposedly returning to India due to unhappiness, likely exacerbated by the racial prejudices of the time. Morag found it strange that there was no trace of her departure, especially as she would have had to travel a considerable distance to Larkhall's East Station.

Katriona's research led her to explore the history of the Lady. Ignoring ghostly tales, she delved into records in London, Edinburgh, and local archives, as well as in the South African Records Office and British military records. She identified the Lady as Sita Phurdeen, born in Ceylon around 1862. Sita, likely from a high-caste background, had moved to South Africa and later worked in the British Army camps. She might have met Captain Henry McNeil-Hamilton there and accompanied him to Scotland in 1902, disguised as a servant or nanny for his children.

In September 1989, Katriona organised an overnight stay at Broomhill House. She and seven women gathered around a fire in the old kitchen, avoiding any mention of the Lady of Larkhall. Around 2am, Mairi needed to find a private outdoor spot. Katriona, with a torch, took her to a secluded area behind the house known as the Lady of Larkhall's Walk. Katriona later recounted what happened:

> "I was holding the light when I heard movement behind me. At first, I thought it was one of the other girls, but then I felt something was off. A terrible cold clung to me, followed by a strong smell of spices, like a bad perfume. A female form passed my left side. I felt frightened but not threatened, and overwhelmingly sad. Mairi asked me to shine the torch, and there was someone standing beside her, with that smell. I shone the torch and saw a shadow on the back wall, moving like someone on a casual walk. I was about 38, the same age Sita would have been when she came to Scotland."

A retired journalist from Cambuslang, researching the town's history, contacted Katriona with surprising news: years ago another Asian woman had disappeared from the Buchanan estate in Cambuslang, some twelve miles away from Larkhall. The woman, linked to McNeil-Hamilton's circle, had travelled by boat to Scotland with Sita.

Intrigued by this news, Katriona enlisted the help of the Scottish Society for Psychical Research to investigate Broomhill. Three clairvoyants, unfamiliar with the lore, each sensed an eerie atmosphere. One detected dark energies, another sensed witchcraft, and one felt a pervasive presence of fire, indicating multiple bodies buried in the cellar.

One clairvoyant described a vivid scene. Though the gatehouse entrance no longer existed, the iron gates still stood either side of the path, and she heard approaching carriages. She then saw a fair-haired woman, reminiscent of McNeil-Hamilton's wife, visibly distressed and clutching her chest. Nearby, a man lay wounded, as if struck by a passing horse. Juxtaposed with this scene, she could see children playing croquet in the background. The clairvoyant noted a resemblance between Katriona and a woman walking beside her, suggesting a connection; the clairvoyant said, "There's a woman walking beside you; she's so like you, you're her double."

Katriona replied, "If it's who I think it is, she had a distinguishing mark."

The clairvoyant then touched her forehead with three fingers. Katriona's grandmother had a permanent mark on her forehead from a fall down the steps at Broomhill. The clairvoyant then described an Asian woman in pain, possibly linked to a violent birth, and advised finding a stone to locate an entrance and a family Bible for a message.

In 1954, while Broomhill was still standing, Jennie MacLeod and friends spent a night there as a dare. Midnight came and went without incident; then at 2am a firecracker thrown by some local kids who'd snuck in to scare the group was thrown. The sudden noise startled the women in their sleeping bags, causing panic, and most ran from the room, but Jennie found herself trapped inside and had to escape by clambering through one of the kitchen windows.

As Jennie fled, she realised that in the confusion and darkness she had run in the wrong direction and ended up at the back of the house. Gathering her thoughts, a chill came over her as something to her side caught her attention. It was then she realised she had come face to face with a tall woman of Asian descent and had almost run straight into her. Jennie noted that the woman had an overpowering smell, a musky scent like the heavy smell of spices. The apparition stared straight at her, eyes fixed on hers, with long slender arms folded across its chest and palms pressed against its shoulders. Slowly, the spirit moved, lowering one hand until the index finger pointed in front of her. At first, Jennie thought she was pointing to their feet, but then she saw the woman was pointing to the ground between them. Soon, Jennie found herself overwhelmed with a sense of dread.

Jennie rushed past the woman and returned home. Later, she told her grandmother, a spey-wife (fortune teller), what had happened and what she'd witnessed; she was urged by her grandmother to return alone to Broomhill. Shortly after, Jennie's grandmother sadly passed, so she felt she owed it to her to go back to the site she'd had such a shock.

Returning to Broomhill, on her own and in the dark, she sat patiently for an hour or so, waiting to see what happened, then the Lady of Larkhall appeared to her again, and again she was pointing, but this time to a slope of land behind Jennie. When she turned round to see why she pointed there, Jennie saw thirteen other figures, some of them children, on the spot where the apparition was gesturing to. For forty years, Jennie kept silent until Katriona's articles brought the story to light and she felt she had to speak of her encounters.

McNeil-Hamilton died in 1924, and by 1937, all valuables had been removed from Broomhill, which had been left to deteriorate. After the 1943 fire, it became semi-derelict and was sold in 1954 to Euphemia Hamilton. Since then, it has been abandoned and falling into ruin.

By the 1960s, the house's most resilient feature was its reputation. A film crew from the BBC's *Tonight* programme, headed by well-known reporter Fyfe Robertson, was allowed into the cellars to attempt a "live" exorcism for the *Tonight* programme. Although they captured no evidence of the paranormal, despite the fine weather on the day of filming, incredibly the cameras, all of them, were found to have completely frozen over, and tragically, after filming finished, the director was killed in a road crash on his way to another location. The impact of the crash threw him from his vehicle, and he was found with a fence post impaled in his heart.

It seems their efforts at exorcism failed.

Wild tales circulated about the vindictive nature of the Lady of Larkhall. A stone lintel weighing several hundredweight was carried by five men from the ruins to be used in the nearby Applebank Inn, and was apparently found the next morning as if it had been hurled from the pub into the middle of the road. Bottles are also said to have exploded in front of shocked patrons, and glasses have flown from the shelves, causing regulars to duck out of the way, to save being hit. It's also said that people passing by the building late at night have heard banging noises from within.

A local ghost-hunter alleged that his back was broken by the lintel, and in May 1995, he claimed the Lady of Larkhall, resenting his meddling, attempted to harm him with a mysterious virus, according to reports in the *News of the World*. However, these sensational accounts contrast sharply with the descriptions provided by others who have encountered the ghost, describing her as more sorrowful and non-threatening.

Members from both sides of Katriona's family have worked at Broomhill. In the 1861 census, she even found a maid named Katriona MacDonald, who was married to a man named James – the same name as her own husband.

If the dream that motivated Katriona's research into the haunting held any meaning, perhaps her grandmother, the "older me" in a white blouse and long black skirt, was trying to communicate something. It seems unlikely that a woman who had served the house so faithfully for many years wouldn't have known if anything suspicious had occurred.

While researching another topic for a heritage society meeting, Katriona stumbled upon a photograph of the Central Station opening in Larkhall in 1905. In the photo was the man from her dream, with piercing eyes. It was Captain Henry McNeil-Hamilton, who had sold some of his land to the Caledonian Railway Co. and was the guest of honour at the ceremony.

The estate owned most of the land and houses in Larkhall, and some of the pits in the area. When McNeil-Hamilton married in 1896, it was one of the biggest society weddings in Lanarkshire, reported in local papers and the *Glasgow Herald*. Bonfires were lit on Tinto and at Broomhill, and some of the great Border families, including the Homes and the Douglases, were represented. The captain's battalion band played on the lawn, the honeymoon was on the Riviera, and gold, diamonds and other jewels were among the sumptuous wedding presents. But when he died, his obituary was a mere eleven words long, and the funeral procession consisted of the hearse and one other car behind it. He was buried with his father in Larkhall Cemetery, but whereas the father's name is on the grave, his son's is not. Something had happened between wedding and funeral – more than just the separation – to make McNeil-Hamilton a shunned figure in Lanarkshire society.

An elderly man, who had once been an apprentice to the local undertaker, shared with Katriona: "One evening we received a call informing us that the laird had died, and we were instructed to bring a coffin to the house immediately. The boss planned to take him away and prepare him. But the laird's son insisted we handle everything there and seal the coffin on the spot. When we went upstairs to his room, the stench was overwhelming, even with the window open. It took me months to regain my appetite." Regardless of what McNeil-Hamilton had done or been accused of during his life, he died a sad and lonely death at fifty-two.

Did Katriona's grandmother witness anything during her time as a servant there? She never spoke of it, but perhaps she felt a need to communicate, visiting Katriona in her dreams.

It's unlikely she noticed nothing, given that servants often have deep insights into their employers' lives. At Broomhill, like many large estates, servants were privy to many secrets. McNeil-Hamilton's brothers had their own scandals: one was a known kleptomaniac, never prosecuted due to his family name; the other was reputedly homosexual and vanished, reportedly to South Africa, never to return.

Some say McNeil-Hamilton was a perfect gentleman, but in Larkhall, many thought otherwise. An old miner recalled climbing the wall at Broomhill as a boy, only to have the laird whip his hands, severing three fingers. A woman remembered pushing her children out of the way when the laird rode by on his black horse, whip in hand, as he never stopped for anyone. Another woman, who worked as a maid at Broomhill, recounted how the maids invited their boyfriends into the kitchen while the laird was away. They stole some of his liquor, watered down the rest, and were having a great time until the laird returned unexpectedly. He was furious, grabbing one man by the neck and throwing him out, and attacking another lad near the cellar. His rage was terrifying; he seemed to lose all control.

Interestingly, the current owner of Broomhill, who has left the land mostly untouched since buying it in 1954, denied any validity of the Lady of Larkhall stories. Despite allowing TV crews to film in the cellars in the 1960s, she later denied the existence of any cellars at Broomhill. When Katriona's research started appearing in the local paper and renewed interest in the ruins, bulldozers were sent to fill in the cellar entrances and destroy the remaining stonework above ground. It seemed an odd response for a place supposedly devoid of mystery or sinister secrets.

As the stories of Broomhill House continue to spread, they serve as a powerful reminder of the weight of history and the mysteries it can leave behind. Whether driven by curiosity, a thirst for the unknown, or a quest for truth, those who explore the secrets of the Lady of Larkhall and the mysterious past of McNeil-Hamilton find themselves immersed in a collection of tales both eerie and captivating. While physical evidence may have disappeared, the legends endure, preserving the past in the minds of those who dare to recall. Only time will tell if these echoes of the past conceal deeper truths or if they will fade away, leaving behind a legacy of unanswered questions and the remnants of a forgotten era.

What happened to Sita? Did she return home, or did she meet a dreadful end at the hands of someone she trusted and travelled across the world to be with? We may never know. Is it possible that the series of dreadful events that befell those who were later involved in this tale were a result of the anger felt by Sita, somehow cursing the building she was so unhappy in?

Whatever the truth, I hope she has now moved on and found the happiness she was so lacking in life.

This story earns its place in my book on overlooked and underreported ghost tales because it offers a fresh perspective on paranormal phenomena often overshadowed by more famous haunts in Edinburgh and the Highlands. After all, the west coast of Scotland has just as much history as any other area. It also has that rare mix of real-life haunting and true crime, with a hint of a curse thrown in.

By highlighting a lesser-known but equally intriguing aspect of Scotland's supernatural lore, this story brings to light the experiences of individuals with a personal connection to the haunting. Their accounts underscore the significance of local ghost stories outside the usual spotlight. By exploring the impact of these encounters on those involved, the story invites readers to consider the rich range of paranormal experiences beyond the well-trodden paths of popular ghost tourism.

CHAPTER 21
ROSSLYN CHAPEL AND ROSLIN CASTLE

THE FIRST WAR of Scottish Independence, which began in 1296 and raged on until 1328, was a time of great turmoil and heroism. It was a period when Scotland fiercely resisted English attempts to dominate the country, and saw legendary figures such as William Wallace and Robert the Bruce rise to prominence, leading their countrymen in a relentless struggle for freedom.

The conflict erupted when King Edward I of England invaded Scotland, determined to bring it under his rule. But the Scots, resolute in their desire for independence, fought back with all their might. The early years of the war were marked by bloody battles, including the Scottish victory at the Battle of Stirling Bridge in 1297, where William Wallace and Andrew Moray defeated a much larger English force.

However, the Scots faced setbacks too, such as the crushing defeat at the Battle of Falkirk, a year later in 1298.

Despite these ups and downs, the Scots never lost their determination and desire for self-governance and national sovereignty.

The war dragged on, with the Scottish people enduring great hardships but refusing to submit. By 1303, the situation was dire. The English had established and captured strongholds throughout Scotland, and the Scottish forces were scattered, depleted in number and weary. Yet hope was not lost. In this desperate hour, Scottish leaders John Comyn and Simon Fraser devised a bold plan.

John Comyn, also known as John "the Red" Comyn, was a prominent Scottish nobleman and Guardian of Scotland, while Simon Fraser was a knight and experienced military leader. Together, they planned a daring assault on the English forces.

On a cold February morning, they gathered their forces near the village of Roslin, just south of Edinburgh. The English army, divided into three separate columns, was marching through the area, overconfident and unaware of the impending danger. This strategy aimed to cover more ground and effectively control the territory, but it also made each column more vulnerable to attack, and the Scots decided to take advantage of this division. The English troops had every reason to be confident, with accounts estimating their numbers to be around thirty thousand men, while the Scots numbered around only eight thousand.

Despite being outnumbered, the Scots commanders, Comyn and Fraser, leveraged their intimate knowledge of the terrain to gain a significant advantage. They strategically utilised the hilly, wooded landscape and the presence of the River Esk to outmanoeuvre and outsmart the larger English force.

The battle began with a sudden assault on the first English column. Caught off guard, the English soldiers were quickly overwhelmed and driven back, with most of them either killed or wounded.

Encouraged by this initial success, the Scots swiftly moved to attack the second column, achieving another decisive victory and claiming thousands of English lives. The final English column, demoralised and disorganised, fell last.

Fifteenth-century Scottish historian John of Fordun wrote a description of the fight in his book *The Chronica Gentis Scotorum*:

> *...there never was so desperate a struggle, or one in which the stoutness of knightly prowess shone forth so brightly. The commander and leader in this struggle was John Comyn, the son... But John Comyn, then guardian of Scotland, and Simon Fraser with their followers, day and night, did their best to harass and to annoy, by their general prowess, the aforesaid kings officers and bailiffs... But the aforesaid John Comyn and Simon, with their abettors, hearing of their arrival, and wishing to steal a march rather than have one stolen upon them, came briskly through from Biggar to Rosslyn, in one night, with some chosen men, who chose rather death before unworthy subjection to the English nation; and all of a sudden they fearlessly fell upon the enemy.*

The Scots had achieved an extraordinary triumph against overwhelming odds with estimates putting the English losses as high as thirty thousand, although this is believed to be an exaggeration based on fifteenth-century retellings of the battle.

The Battle of Roslin was a remarkable episode in the First War of Scottish Independence, a testament to the courage and ingenuity of the Scottish forces. It demonstrated that even in the darkest of times, the Scots were capable of remarkable feats, driven by their unwavering desire for freedom.

Amidst the aftermath of this historic battle, on the outskirts of the village of Roslin, Rosslyn Chapel and Castle stand as symbols of the area's rich history and mystery. Before these structures existed, the land was home to an ancient church dedicated to St Peter, serving the local community.

Rosslyn Castle's history dates back to the early 1300s when it was initially constructed as a timber structure by the Sinclair family, a prominent Scottish noble lineage. Originating from France, the Sinclairs, also known as the St Clares, have held Roslin since 1280. Over time, the castle underwent gradual reconstruction and expansion, evolving into a formidable stone fortress.

Throughout Scottish history, it played a pivotal role, witnessing various conflicts, including the Wars of Scottish Independence.

Today, much of Rosslyn Castle lies in ruins after being subjected to heavy artillery fire from Cromwell's army in 1650; when they'd finished, they left just the buttress still standing. However, some parts have been restored and are still inhabited.

Rosslyn Chapel, officially the Collegiate Chapel of St Matthew, was founded in 1446 by Sir William Sinclair, 1st Earl of Caithness. The chapel was meant to be a place of worship and a collegiate church, where prayers would be said for the souls of the Sinclair family.

Although construction continued for nearly forty years, it was never completed as originally planned. The original plans included designs for a nave and a tower, which were never completed. These unfinished parts remain as they were during the construction period, providing insight into the ambitious architectural vision that was never fully realised.

Despite this, Rosslyn Chapel is celebrated for its intricate and symbolic carvings, which have inspired numerous legends and theories.

Perhaps the most well-known carving within the chapel has come to be known as "the Apprentice Pillar".

The Apprentice Pillar, also known as the "Prentice Pillar", stands as a masterpiece of mediaeval stone carving, loved for its intricate design and symbolic significance, and according to legend, the pillar holds a tale of tragedy, inspiration, and remarkable craftsmanship.

There are many legends as to its origins, but the one that has stuck with me most tells of its creation during the fifteenth century. As the story goes, the master mason responsible for overseeing the construction of Rosslyn Chapel was tasked with designing a pillar of unparalleled beauty. However, the mason fell ill before completing his work, leaving the apprentice to carry out the intricate carving in his absence.

Inspired by a vision or dream, the apprentice began carving the pillar, pouring his heart and soul into every detail. Legend has it that the design he created was so exquisite and intricate that it surpassed even the master mason's expectations. However, upon returning from his illness, the master mason was consumed by jealousy and rage upon seeing the apprentice's masterpiece.

In a fit of jealous fury, the master mason struck down the apprentice, killing him on the spot. It is said that the apprentice's blood stained the stone pillar, leaving a permanent mark that can still be seen today. Some versions of the legend suggest that the master mason was so remorseful for his actions that he carved his own face into the opposite side of the pillar as a tribute to the apprentice's skill and dedication.

Regardless of the specifics of the legend, the Apprentice Pillar stands as a remarkable example of the skill and craftsmanship of the mediaeval artisans responsible for constructing Rosslyn Chapel.

This murderous act has echoed through the ages, and the spirit of the slain apprentice has been reportedly seen standing near the masterpiece that would cost him his life.

Another of the most enduring legends associated with Rosslyn Chapel is its supposed connection to the Knights Templar. This mediaeval Christian military order was known for its role in the Crusades and its mysterious disappearance. Some theories suggest that the Sinclair family, who had ties to the Templars, incorporated Templar symbolism and secrets into the chapel's design. These theories include the possibility that the chapel was a repository for Templar treasures or even the Holy Grail. Though these claims lack historical evidence, they have fueled popular imagination and speculation.

Even before Rosslyn Chapel was built, the site was believed to hold spiritual significance, possibly used by the Templars or earlier religious groups. The exact nature of this earlier use remains a subject of debate among historians and archaeologists.

Rosslyn Chapel and Castle continue to captivate visitors with their historical and architectural significance. The chapel, in particular, gained international fame through its inclusion in Dan Brown's novel *The Da Vinci Code,* which brought renewed attention to its mysterious carvings and Templar connections.

Today, both Rosslyn Chapel and Castle remain important cultural and historical landmarks, drawing tourists and researchers alike who seek to unravel their secrets and appreciate their beauty, and both sites are said to be haunted.

In July 2006, as the Edinburgh Festival drew near, a group of young actors, filled with excitement, gathered in Rosslyn Chapel to rehearse for their upcoming performance. Amidst the ancient stone walls, their voices echoed with the promise of theatrical magic.

As the rehearsal reached its crescendo, one actor, a young man in his early twenties, paused, his attention caught by a shimmering, seemingly spectral figure that could be seen flitting through the grounds of the chapel. It danced with ethereal grace, its form reminiscent of a fairy from tales of old. Though others dismissed it as a trick of the light, the actor remained transfixed, sensing something supernatural in its presence.

Later that evening, as the last echoes of their performance faded and the sun began to dip below the horizon, another actor found himself left with the task of locking up the chapel alone. Just as he was about to secure the doors, a faint sound permeated the silence. At first he put it down to his friends carrying on their rehearsals as they packed up their equipment, but the sound that reached his ears was different, so he stopped what he was doing, putting the keys in his pocket to stop any jingling, and listened intently – the noise came again, this time louder, closer and clearer, and this time he knew it wasn't his friends, it was the laughter of a child, echoing from the depths of the cold, dark crypt below.

Naturally concerned that a child might be trapped inside, he hurried down into the dimly lit chamber. But as he descended the stone steps into the crypt's shadowy embrace, the laughter faded into silence. The crypt lay empty, devoid of any sign of life. Bewildered but convinced at what he'd heard, the actor searched every corner, every shadow, but found no trace of the elusive child.

Perplexed and unsettled, he returned to his friends, who were enjoying the last of the fresh air and watching bats as they began their nocturnal flight. Despite his attempts to shake off the mysterious encounter, the memory of the laughter lingered in his mind, and he was compelled to tell his friend.

As his tale unfolded, the other actors huddled together, exchanging murmurs of speculation. Was it a mere figment of his imagination, sparked by the eerie atmosphere of the chapel? Or had the fleeting encounter been a glimpse into the realm of the supernatural? Perhaps the solitary actor, entrusted with securing the ancient site, had also stumbled upon something truly otherworldly within the sacred confines of Rosslyn Chapel.

As the group left for the night, the mystery of that summer evening remained.

For as long as it has stood, Rosslyn Chapel has been a sanctuary for monks, a sacred refuge where prayers ascended like incense to the heavens. Yet some say that not all who sought solace within its walls departed in peace.

Local legends tell of monks whose spirits linger still, their ghostly forms bound to the chapel's ancient stones. Among them, a lone ghostly figure seemingly stands vigil at the crypt's altar, his transparent form illuminated by flickering candlelight at night or sunlight passing through the stained-glass windows during the day. Witnesses recount a solitary monk deeply immersed in prayer, with head bowed and hands clasped in devout reverence. He appears lost in a timeless reverie, oblivious to the mortal world around him, embodying Rosslyn Chapel's enduring sanctity.

On several occasions when he has been witnessed by unsuspecting staff and visitors, he is not alone; four phantom knights stand silently beside him. No one has yet been able to identify the figures or why they appear alongside the monk, which adds to the mystery of their presence.

Who could these knights be? Given the chapel's links to the Knights Templar, is it possible they have a link to this historic order, or could they be members of the Sinclair fighting force? Perhaps they are simply warriors of old, praying for protection before riding off into a battle they may never have returned from.

In 2010, workmen undertook some overnight work within the chapel. However, after three separate groups completed their overnight shifts, all unanimously vowed never to return for night work there.

While many remained tight-lipped about their reasons, one worker recounted feeling an unusual sensation while repairing the steps leading to the crypt. He sensed a presence behind him and, upon turning, spotted a monk garbed in a brown cassock observing him. Startled, he swiftly exited the premises and urged the night watchman to inspect the area, yet no monk was to be found.

Throughout the ages, countless souls have also reported mysterious noises echoing throughout the chapel's walls. Some speculate that these eerie sounds could be the echoes of centuries-old rituals performed by monks in solemn devotion. Others suggest that they may be the restless whispers of spirits trapped between worlds, their presence haunting the sacred space. Yet the true origin of these enigmatic sounds remains a puzzle, shrouded in the mists of time, awaiting discovery by those brave enough to unravel its secrets.

While Rosslyn Chapel is world famous for its secrets and mysteries, the nearby castle is equally remarkable, boasting its very own supernatural secrets.

On the Sinclair family's ancestral land, beneath the looming presence of the castle's remains, tales are told of a mysterious, imposing figure. Passed down through generations, these stories tell of a spectral rider, shrouded in darkness and mounted on a huge black phantom horse, who is seen in the woods around the castle and seemingly patrolling the roads leading to the castle.

Often sightings of him are preceded by the heavy, rhythmic hoofbeats of his mighty horse before he comes into view and terrifies those unfortunate enough to witness him.

It was on the winding roads that skirt the castle's domain that motorists, unsuspecting travellers of the modern age, first encountered the apparition. Three separate occasions bore witness to the ghostly manifestation of a black knight on horseback, his spectral form materialising to horrified witnesses in the dead of night.

Within the Sinclair family, the stories of the haunting became ingrained in their history, becoming a part of their heritage. While the identity of the phantom rider remains unknown, speculation thrives among those intrigued by the mysteries of the past.

Some believe he is a knight from the distant past, lost in the chaos of battle long ago. Others think he watches over the land, bound by duty or an unfinished task.

But whatever the theories, one fact is clear: the legend of the black knight persists, adding to the mysteries of the Sinclair estate.

There are stories of a spectral presence that haunts the ancient halls of Rosslyn Castle – the ghost of a white lady.

It is said that she was once a maiden of the St Clair family, ensnared by an evil spell cast upon her by dark forces. She sleeps in an enchanted chamber, awaiting the touch of a noble knight to break the curse that binds her.

Another, somewhat less romantic version of her story suggests she was a maid responsible for looking after the St Clair children at the castle. According to this account, she became frightened by a mouse, accidentally dropped her candle, and started a fire. Tragically, she perished in the flames. It is said that her ghost has been sighted in the castle, holding her candle.

A third version of the story suggests that within the ancient castle lies a hidden treasure, protected by a figure known as the "White Lady". Local legend holds that she can only be roused and the treasure uncovered by sounding a trumpet while standing on a specific step of one of the staircases.

Over the generations, her story has evolved, each retelling adding fresh details. Some claim that the knight who saves her will be rewarded with great wealth, their destinies entwined in a tale of fate. I've often wondered if anyone has tried to break her enchantment and claim the prize the legend promises.

The locals of Roslin say the ghost of the white lady still watches silently, reminding us of the enduring themes of love and redemption.

The oldest tale associated with the castle tells of the haunting of the woods by a phantom hound, its mournful howls piercing the darkness on stormy nights. According to legend, detailed in R. Robertson MacDonald's *More Highland Folktales,* the story dates back to a fateful encounter on February 24, 1303.

During the bloody battle of Roslin Glen, an English knight, accompanied by his formidable war hound, fell at the hands of a Scottish soldier. Enraged, the hound turned on its master's killer, prompting the Scotsman to frantically defend himself by slaying the beast.

That night, within the walls of Roslin Castle, the ghostly apparition of the hound materialised in the guardroom, sending waves of terror through the soldiers who witnessed it. Henceforth, the spectral canine made nightly appearances, earning the moniker "Mauthe Doog" among the troops. One evening, it was the turn of the soldier who had dispatched the hound's master to stand guard. As he patrolled the castle's corridors with the keys in hand, he was confronted by the menacing snarls of the phantom hound. Overwhelmed with fear, he let out a piercing scream before fleeing in blind panic. He never recovered from the ordeal, succumbing to silence and passing away three days later. Though the hound vanished from the castle thereafter, the haunting echoes of its baying persist to this day.

A more modern account happened in the twentieth century and was recounted by a local man named John Ritchie. He recounted:

> "I was born and brought up in Roslin and went to school in the village. When I was about twelve years old, my friend Neil and I spent quite a bit of time playing in Roslin

Castle, as Neil's aunt was the caretaker and lived in the castle some forty years ago. We explored most of the nooks and crannies of the castle, as boys of that age are wont to do.

"One Saturday, near the end of February (my birthday is the 25th of February, this is why I remember it), we were exploring the second-level corridor, which connects the monks' cells, the old scriptorium, and the dungeons, when all of a sudden we were aware of some light coming from the end of the corridor which had had the windows blocked up, and there was normally no light coming from that area. The light grew in intensity, which was enough to alarm the senses of two twelve-year-olds, who admittedly were searching for just this kind of experience.

"We both looked at each other to check that we were both aware of the phenomenon; we both turned at the same time and took off along the corridor at what seemed like record-breaking speed, until we came to the old main kitchen, which is a big room with a stone staircase, which is built into the right-hand side or the east wall of the castle. As we hurried up the stair, we looked down to see the light, which had been growing and moving towards us down the corridor, was what appeared to be a large wolfhound-type dog, which ran underneath us and appeared to go straight through the wall next to the large fireplace, which was the old main cooking area for the castle. We did not stop until we got up the staircase and through the door into the upper part of the castle.

"To be suddenly met by Neil's aunt, who could tell from our nervous state that something had happened. When we blurted out the story, Neil's aunt smiled and said, 'Aye, boys, it's an old castle, with lots of strange things like that, but

> dinna worry about them, they will no harm ye. Come and have a bottle of lemonade.'
>
> "Nothing more was said, we drank our lemonade and had some biscuits, and the sense of fear dropped away. But we did not go near that particular corridor for quite a long time.
>
> "Much later we looked at the wall where the apparition of the dog had disappeared to find that it had once been a doorway. The arch from the door still exists today. Neil's aunt lived at the castle on her own for about twenty years as the sole caretaker and tourist guide, and many times recently, I have wished that I had spoken more to her about her experiences at the castle, but youth rejects the wisdom of age, and it's only now I regret missing the opportunities gifted to youth."

I have included the ghost stories of Rosslyn Chapel and Roslin Castle in this book to shed light on the lesser-known aspects of these historic sites. While Rosslyn Chapel is world famous for its enigmatic symbolism, history and intricate architecture, its reputation as a haunted location remains, surprisingly, relatively obscure. Similarly, historic Roslin Castle, often overshadowed by the chapel's fame, holds its own mysterious, haunting tales that deserve recognition.

One of my favourite types of ghosts featured in these stories is the "white lady". I've always been drawn to tales of "white ladies" such as the white lady of Roslin Castle; they appear in many classic hauntings and create a truly evocative image. I can vividly recall my childhood fear of venturing into the woods near our first house in Mortonhall, a housing estate to the south of Edinburgh, especially when the ball inevitably ended up there during a game of football. I was the goalkeeper, so responsibility lay with me if someone had a shot and the ball went past me and into the woods.

My young and perhaps overly active imagination was filled with tales of the "white lady of Mortonhall", a ghostly figure said to roam the woods day and night, lurking behind trees and waiting to capture and spirit away, to who knows where, unsuspecting children who ventured in search of their footballs. This gave me added incentive to prevent anyone from scoring – I certainly didn't want to go into those woods.

Looking back, I'm convinced now that this story was concocted to keep us away from the woods and off the private land of Mortonhall House. However, at that age, it was a genuine concern and not something I was willing to test.

While some of these tales may carry a cautionary tone, my exploration of these ghostly legends aims to enrich the histories of both Rosslyn Chapel and Roslin Castle. By delving into these stories, I hope to offer a fresh perspective on their mysteries and historical significance, revealing new insights into the allure that continues to fascinate visitors and historians.

CHAPTER 22
CLOSING

FOR AS LONG AS I can remember, I've been truly captivated by ghost stories. I've come to realise that the only thing that completely engrosses me and captures my attention is a well-told ghost story. When I hear or read one, it feels like the rest of the world switches off. Growing up in Edinburgh, a city steeped in history, often violent and macabre history, and mystery, tales of the supernatural were as much a part of my upbringing as the cobbled streets and ancient castles.

I have fond memories of sitting in our kitchen in Mortonhall in the early '80s, listening intently as my mother regaled me with her favourite horror movies like *Rosemary's Baby*. Her storytelling prowess brought these tales to life, and I can still recall the thrill of fear that ran down my spine as she spun her yarns. Even my sister, after watching *Salem's Lot* during a weekend stay with our grandparents, added to the atmosphere of haunting delight. I soon came to the realisation that it wasn't the blood and gore that fascinated me, but rather the art of storytelling itself – the way a well-crafted ghost or horror story could give me goose-bumps and linger in my imagination long after the tale had ended.

My father would also tell me of a glowing, green ghostly highwayman he encountered while working in Northern Ireland. This really struck a chord with me, as this was the first time I knew someone who claimed to have seen a ghost "in the flesh". This experience, although not mine, brought the paranormal out of Hollywood and into the real world for me.

But my favourite *ghost* story was something that happened to my mum when she was a youngster. My grandparents lived in the Gilmerton area of Edinburgh, and behind their house was a farmer's field imaginatively known as "the Field", with a small copse of trees on the far side of the field. My mother and her friends had been out playing in the field as darkness began to fall – this was back in the days when you went out when the sun came up, and came back home when it went down – when one of the girls saw a white figure moving in the trees in the distance. The girls hightailed it out of the field and ran screaming for their dads, who dutifully came running to investigate.

They inched their way towards the trees, torches and sticks in hand. The white figure was spotted again, so most people ran towards it; some ran away. As they drew closer to the figure, it became clear it was…a black and white cow. The dads had a good laugh, and the girls, though embarrassed, were relieved it wasn't something more sinister. This story has been told countless times at family gatherings, a reminder that sometimes our imaginations can run wild, especially in the dim light of dusk. Despite the anticlimactic yet humorous ending, it remains my favourite ghost story, illustrating how easily the mind can be tricked and how the simplest explanations are often the most unexpected.

Over the years, my love for ghost stories and the paranormal has only deepened, leading me on a journey to uncover the forgotten and overlooked tales of Scotland's haunted past. Through my research with Eerie Edinburgh, I've unearthed layers of hauntings that expanded my understanding, stumbling upon truly captivating encounters, many of which were entirely new to me.

These findings underscore Scotland's enduring love for mysteries and the paranormal, a fascination deeply ingrained in the Scottish psyche – after all, what other country would choose a mythical creature like the unicorn as its national animal? This symbol embodies our love for the enigmatic and unexplained. Moreover, these stories remind us of humanity's timeless intrigue with the mysterious. In our contemporary era, where science often seeks to demystify the world, these tales persist, inviting us to explore the shadows and share the wonders we uncover.

Since starting Eerie Edinburgh, I've discovered a burgeoning community of storytellers, such as John Tantalon and Kerrie Powell from North Edinburgh Nightmares, Graeme Milne, and Scott Lyal, who share my passion for keeping these tales alive. With this book, I aim to preserve some of these stories and contribute to the ongoing preservation of Scotland's rich supernatural heritage.

I hope that these tales and encounters encourage people to look beyond the Edinburgh Vaults and Greyfriars Kirkyard, exploring further afield to truly experience the depth of Scotland's hauntings and mysteries. While these are undoubtedly fascinating locations that hold an undeniable place in Edinburgh's history, there are equally intriguing sites waiting to be discovered. For instance, if you want to explore an unusual underground location, travel to the old mining village of Gilmerton on the outskirts of the city, where you'll find Gilmerton Cove – a series of hand-carved underground passages and chambers with mysterious origins and a reputation for being haunted.

There is so much more to discover, from remote villages to ancient castles, each with its own captivating stories waiting to be uncovered.

Lastly, I hope that I can help people feel they can be open in sharing their own stories and experiences. As I previously mentioned, I'm convinced almost everyone has had a weird encounter or knows someone who does. By sharing these accounts, not only do we gain insights into our history, but as part of a collective discussion, we can also better understand specific aspects of hauntings, such as why the ghostly apparition in Bearsden may have had sharp teeth. If you have a story to share or are curious about such phenomena, I encourage you to reach out to individuals like myself who are committed to respectfully exploring and sharing these narratives.

In conclusion, my journey into Scotland's supernatural realm has deepened my appreciation for the unknown. From Edinburgh's narrow cobbled streets to the vast openness of the Scottish Highlands, tales of hauntings have enriched my understanding of our cultural heritage. Through my work with Eerie Edinburgh, I've encountered a vibrant community of storytellers dedicated to preserving these narratives. Together, we stand at the intersection of past and present, embracing the mysteries of the paranormal.

As I finish this exploration, I hold a deep respect for Scotland's haunted past and the enduring fascination of its incredible haunting tales.

Want more Hidden Haunts?

Hidden Haunts: England
Hidden Haunts: Ireland

ABOUT THE AUTHOR

Born in the atmospheric city of Edinburgh in the 1970s, Wayne Gilbert is a storyteller whose passion for the eerie and mysterious was sparked from a young age. Surrounded by the historic and haunted streets of Edinburgh, Wayne's fascination with classic ghost stories grew alongside his exploration of books like *The Hamlyn Book of Horror* and the works of Peter Underwood. These early influences ignited Wayne's journey into the realm of the supernatural.

Guided by a lifelong fascination with the paranormal, Wayne has evolved into a captivating storyteller, adept at weaving narratives that bridge the gap between the seen and the unseen. The enchanting landscapes and rich history of his birthplace have deepened his connection to the ghostly, offering a unique perspective on the spectral tales that haunt the corners of Edinburgh and Scotland.

As the curator of the YouTube channel Eerie Edinburgh, Wayne passionately shares the haunted history of Edinburgh and beyond, bringing enigmatic stories of the supernatural to a global audience. His work invites viewers and readers alike to explore the lesser-known and overlooked tales of Edinburgh and Scotland's most hauntingly beautiful locations.

For personal stories or inquiries, contact Wayne at
contact@eerieedinburgh.com

For more ghostly tales and spooky stories, visit:
www.eerieedinburgh.com

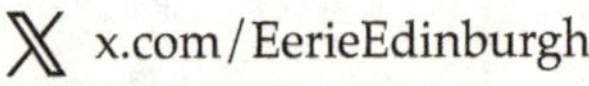

instagram.com/Eerie_Edinburgh

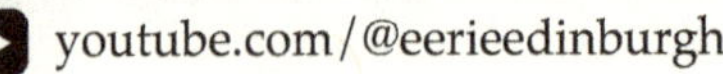

Prepare to embark on a hauntingly thrilling journey into the mysterious world of Scotland's spectral inhabitants with our channel, "Eerie Edinburgh." We are your portal to the eerie, the unexplained, and the spine-tingling stories that have lingered in the shadows of Scotland for generations.

Join us as we explore the dark, cobblestone streets of Edinburgh, where restless spirits wander through the city's ancient alleyways and historic buildings. Our mission is to bring Scotland's ghostly legends to life, with a particular focus on the enchanting and enigmatic city of Edinburgh.

From the ghostly tales of castles, manors, and historic sites to chilling encounters with apparitions and unexplained phenomena, "Eerie Edinburgh" is your definitive source for all things supernatural. Whether you're a passionate paranormal enthusiast, a history buff, or simply someone seeking an electrifying thrill, our channel promises to keep you on the edge of your seat.

Visit: www.youtube.com/@eerieedinburgh

www.ingramcontent.com/pod-product-compliance
Lightning Source LLC
Chambersburg PA
CBHW032349280326
41935CB00008B/505

* 9 7 8 1 9 5 4 5 2 8 8 6 4 *